TEACHING MUSIC EFFECTIVELY IN THE ELEMENTARY SCHOOL

LOIS CHOKSY

The University of Calgary

PRENTICE HALL, Upper Saddle River, New Jersey 07458

Library of Congress Cataloging-in-Publication Data

CHOKSY, LOIS.
  Teaching music effectively in the elementary school/Lois Choksy.
    p. cm.
  ISBN 0-13-892704-9
  1. School music-Instruction and study. I. Title.
MT1.C5374 1991   90-49554
372.87-dc20   CIP
                                                   MN

Editorial/production supervision
  and interior design: Carole R. Crouse
Cover design: Ray Lundgren Graphics, Ltd.
Prepress buyer: Herb Klein
Manufacturing buyer: Dave Dickey
Acquisitions editor: Norwell Therien

Printed in the United States of America

10 9 8 7 6 5 4 3 2 1

ISBN 0-13-892704-9

Prentice-Hall International (UK) Limited,London
Prentice-Hall of Australia Pty. Limited, Sydney
Prentice-Hall Canada Inc., Toronto
Prentice-Hall Hispanoamericana, S.A., Mexico
Prentice-Hall of India Private Limited, New Delhi
Prentice-Hall of Japan, Inc., Tokyo
Pearson Education Asia Pte. Ltd., Singapore
Editora Prentice-Hall do Brasil, Ltda., Rio de Janeiro

To my dearest friend,
closest professional colleague,
and frankest critic,
NASLI H. CHOKSY

CONTENTS

PREFACE

The *school* is essentially an artificial institution; in the history of mankind, it is a comparatively recent substitute for the old customs of tutors for the titled and wealthy, apprenticeships for skilled workers, and the passing of life-skills from father to son and mother to daughter among agrarian and seafaring peoples.

The environment for learning in earlier times was commonly the real-world environment. An apprentice silversmith worked with the experienced silversmith in his shop. The nobleman's son learned to do battle by serving as a page to a knight going into battle. The nobleman's daughter stayed at home with her mother and learned to sing and play musical instruments and to create pictures of the life around her with her needle. The peasant's son helped in the fields or with the fishing boats while his daughter helped her mother with bread baking and child rearing.

Life was so structured that it was difficult, if not impossible, for an individual to break out of what must have seemed a "preordained" role. The stereotypes of what education should be were dictated both by class and by sex and were questioned by few.

Even when "schools" began to be established as places where the young could be sent to learn to read and write and calculate, the only young sent were males, and the only males sent were sons of the "upper classes." Education as an equal right of all men and women is an idea still in its infancy. The institution we know as the "school" today has taken on all the tasks set for both sexes and all classes in earlier times. The principal environment for learning is no longer the court, the home, the field, the sea, the shop, but a room with desks, books, and a "teacher." And the subject matter studied is all that went before, compounded by all that continues to be discovered, invented, or developed.

There has been among educators a growing realization that it is impossible to teach everything, that children can never learn all the facts or acquire all the skills implied by the ever-growing body of knowledge. Recurring attempts to reduce this mammoth curriculum to "the basics" have usually focused on the first "basics" taught in the earliest schools—reading, writing, 'rithmetic—with little regard for the fact that in the last decade of the twentieth century, these skills are less needed than they have ever been. One is compelled to ask, "For whom are these subjects *basic*?" Such mathematical skills as will ever be needed by the average adult in a computerized world could be taught before the age of nine. Operation of a word processor would surely be a more useful skill in the twenty-first century than handwriting, and while one would hope that reading and writing will continue to be valued as skills, it is impossible to refute the fact that far more adults watch television today than ever read books.

More "reading, writing, and calculating" (with the implication of less of everything else) is surely not the best way to arrive at an appropriate curriculum for today's youth.

If one fact seems certain, it is that the average person today spends decreasing amounts of time earning a living. For many people, hours of "free" time equal or exceed hours spent working. With the advances being made in technology, this trend is unlikely to be reversed.

What, then, should the schools be teaching? What should be the *basics* of the twenty-first century?

Certainly, schools should continue to prepare people for life. But life itself has so changed in the last hundred years that it is obvious that curriculum choices must be made wider, not narrower.

New "basics" are needed—perhaps, instead of "reading and writing," something called "communication skills," which would allow for instruction more in accordance with technological innovations.

But equally basic in a curriculum for the twenty-first century must be provision for instruction in the arts. Only through the arts can teachers counteract the dehumanizing effects of technology.

Acting, drawing, singing, dancing, and playing instruments afford children some of the most rewarding opportunities for interacting with others in school situations in which they are increasingly isolated behind machines.

If men and women are to survive as thinking, caring, feeling beings, then there must be new basics, and prominent among these must be the arts.

Music is basic.

I should like to acknowledge Robert E. Nye (University of Oregon), Hilary Apfelstadt (University of North Carolina), and John W. Flohr (Texas Woman's University) for their prepublication reviews. I feel that this book has been greatly improved by the incorporation of their valuable suggestions.

Lois Choksy

I

TEACHING AND LEARNING THROUGH MUSICAL ACTIVITIES

Children learn by doing. Children learn music by singing, moving, playing instruments, listening, reading, writing, and creating. These are the activities through which children acquire musical skills.

Through these activities, they also come to understand music, to infer concepts about each of the elements of music: melody, duration, form, harmony, tempo, timbre, and dynamics.

The person who understands music—that is, holds valid concepts about the elements of music, and who is skillful in the activities of music will probably hold good attitudes toward music.

It is the function of the teacher to present musical experiences through which children can infer music concepts, develop musical skills, and knowledgeably enjoy the aesthetic experience of music.

This book is organized to assist in that task. Part I is devoted to the experiences through which children learn music. Part II discusses each of the elements of music, with emphasis on the major learnings or concepts necessary for understanding music.

The final chapter suggests ways of organizing these experiences into a framework for teaching.

This book is intended for anyone who ever has to teach music in the schools. While musical background is certainly desirable for such teaching, the author fully realizes that many teachers who are expected to carry on a music program with their classes have little music training or experience to bring to their teaching. This book is presented as a practical guide for such teachers.

CHAPTER 1

WHY SHOULD WE TEACH MUSIC?

Music, one of the oldest and most natural expressions of mankind—as old, perhaps, as language—has been considered by most civilizations to be worthy of being passed from generation to generation. As a part of the cultural heritage of peoples, it has found its way into the educational institutions of many diverse societies.

The ancient Greeks (1200–146 B.C.) considered it a "basic" subject, essential to the educated person. Hebrews used music in religious services long before the advent of Christianity and considered it a cornerstone of education. Egyptian artifacts dating from 4000 B.C. lead musicologists to believe that song and dance occupied an important place in Egyptian life, and primitive cave drawings show even earlier uses of music in people's lives.[1]

But is music relevant to life today? At the dawn of the twenty-first century, in a technological society far removed from the simple needs of cave dwellers, ancient Egyptians, Hebrews, or Greeks, should music occupy a place in the education of the young? If so, what should that place be?

While music itself has changed and continues to change, its role in peoples' lives has not changed markedly since the first cave dwellers banged out a pleasing rhythm on a log.

People use music to celebrate, to mark rites of passage—births, weddings, deaths—to express religious and patriotic feelings, to relax and have a good time, to feel uplifted. They express music through listening to or participating in church choirs, rock groups, oratorio societies, community bands and orchestras, folk music clubs, opera associations, and dance groups, and in countless other ways. Music surrounds present-day life. It is everpresent—in food stores and shopping malls, in restaurants and cafes, on the other end of the telephone when one is put on "hold." There is an enormous commercial market in videocassettes devoted to popular music; there are music festivals of worldwide interest in Bayreuth, Salzburg,

---

[1]Donald H. Van Ess, *The Heritage of Musical Style* (New York: Holt, Rinehart & Winston, 1970), pp. 23–24; and Donald Jay Grout, *A History of Western Music* (New York: W. W. Norton & Co., Inc., 1960), pp. 3–34.

Interlaken, and Glyndebourne; more than 70 percent of radio time is devoted to music; more people attend concerts of one type or another than attend baseball games.

It is obvious that music is still very much a part of life in the last decade of the twentieth century. But does that necessarily mean that music should be a part of curriculum? Does music possess educative value?

THE PLACE OF MUSIC IN EDUCATION

Music should be a part of the education of the young today for a number of reasons; its potential entertainment and recreational value; its career possibilities; its possible effect on self-image and, through this, its contribution to the learning of other life skills; its unique value to holistic education; its socializing influence; its capacity for offering spiritual or uplifting experiences.

Some of these are obviously more concrete and more easily supported by documentation than others; that does not make the other, less tangible reasons less valid. They may actually be the most important reasons for the inclusion of music in the curriculum.

Music as Entertainment and as Recreation

At first glance, these two words, *entertainment* and *recreation,* might seem synonymous. Actually, they imply quite different musical experiences. For the former, education, although desirable, is not necessary; for the latter, education is essential.

Being entertained by music can be a relatively passive activity. Someone else is doing the work. The "receiver" is merely in the presence of that work, in person or by means of radio, video, or sound system. The "receiver" may enjoy the results of the work but is not actively involved in producing those results. However, even at this level, education may play a role. People like best what they know best. The adult who has been fortunate enough to receive a good music education is likely to enjoy a far wider spectrum of musics than the person whose musical experience has been more limited.

Recreational music, on the other hand, involves the receiver in some level of activity. The very word implies action—to re-create. Recreational musical experiences may range from moving rhythmically to music (dancing) to participation in music making (amateur orchestra, band, chorus; pop group; folk club; and so on). For effective participation in any of these, music education is necessary.

Music as a Career

Never before have there been as many or as varied career possibilities in music as there are today. In addition to expanding opportunities in the traditional fields of musical performance and teaching, careers also exist in the areas of music publishing, arts administration, composing, conducting, music journalism, artist management, music therapy, music librarianship, music criticism, church music, orchestra management, radio and television music programming, manufacturing and sales of musical instruments, record disc and tape production, and music research.[2]

---

[2]For further career suggestions see "Career Education in Music," "Careers in Music," and "A Wider View of Music Professions," *Music Educators Journal,* March 1977; and Betty Stearns and Clara Degen (eds.), *Careers in Music* (Wilmette, Ill.: American Music Conference, 1980).

For any career involving music, music education is a requirement. That education should be supplied, at least in part, by the schools, as it is for other careers. No mathematician is expected to acquire all of his knowledge of mathematics in private lessons and at his own expense.

Music and Self-Image

Considerable research has been done in recent years on the role of music in facilitating learning in other areas of curriculum.[3] One thesis, while by no means uncontested, is that through improving the child's self-image, music may play an important role in helping the child to learn other things more easily. Dr. Robert Roy, chief clinical psychologist at the Bosco Home for Boys, quotes some interesting and impressive findings regarding disturbed adolescents who, once taught to sing, were able to read. In another study involving several hundred children in San Jose, California,[4] among the most telling findings were those involving the importance of music to children's self-image, as perceived by the teachers and the parents of the children.

It is not surprising that a child who is taught to sing and is praised for his or her singing should have a more positive self-image as a result. One's voice is deeply personal. To feel that it is "good," that one performs well with it, would seem logically to color one's whole feeling about self. There is ample evidence to show that people who feel good about themselves learn more easily than people whose self-images are negative.

Music and Holistic Education

There has been a great deal written in recent years on brain research and hemispheric dominance. According to psychologists, the left and right hemispheres of the brain serve different functions, the left dealing with analytical, logical thinking, and the right with holistic, intuitive thinking. Left brain is supposedly concerned with speech, sequencing, calculating, cause-and-effect, while right brain is visual-spatial-artistic.[5] The left hemisphere controls the right side of the body, while the right hemisphere controls the left side of the body.

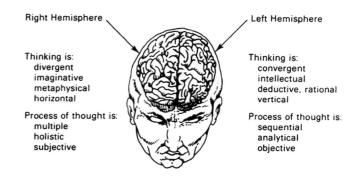

Right Hemisphere   Left Hemisphere

Thinking is:
  divergent
  imaginative
  metaphysical
  horizontal

Thinking is:
  convergent
  intellectual
  deductive, rational
  vertical

Process of thought is:
  multiple
  holistic
  subjective

Process of thought is:
  sequential
  analytical
  objective

[3]Ruth Zinzar, "Reading, Writing, and Music," *Education Summary*, 26, no. 13 (January 1974), 8; Lisa Kuhmarker, "Music in the Beginning Reading Program," *Young Children*, 24, no. 3 (January 1969), 157–63; and Eila Peterson, "Transfer Effects from Music Literacy Training within a Kodály Curriculum Framework to Achievement in Language Reading" (M. Mus. Thesis, The University of Calgary, 1986).

[4]Randolfo R. Pozos, "Kodály Music Education Program: Holy Names College and the San Jose Unified School District" (Oakland, Calif.: Holy Names College, July 1, 1980, Unpublished evaluation report).

[5]This is somewhat simplistic. Research has shown instances in which right-brain functions were assumed by left brain, and vice versa. See Timothy B. Rogers, "Music and Neuropsychology," *Notes*, 8 (1983), 9–16.

In applying the findings of brain research to educational theory, both researchers and teachers have made generalizations as to which subjects are "left brain" (language, science, mathematics) and which are "right brain" (music, art, dance). It quickly becomes apparent that the school has for many years concerned itself primarily with left-brain development. Surely, if there are two sides to the brain, the development of both should be the responsibility of any comprehensive program of education. However, the reality is more complex. Mathematics is not solely a function of the left hemisphere—if it were, there would be no creative theories of mathematics—and music is not solely a right-brain function—if it were, people would not be able to read music. Music is both a right- and a left-brain function.

Dr. Joan MacLeod[6] has made the point that "all experience is thought" and that "every thought can be made visual through symbols." She lists the symbol systems as five: word, number, gesture, image, and sound. Schools deal almost exclusively with the first two of these, word and number. The last three, gesture, image, and sound, are the symbol systems of the arts. No education that ignores them can be considered complete. The schools have a responsibility to help students develop skills in all symbol systems.

Music as a Socializing Influence

Increasingly, in the age of technology, people are isolated from one another. Today, individual computer terminals are being used in many schools to assist learning in spelling, mathematics, language, and other subjects. "Computer literacy" is considered an important goal in many school systems. The next decade will very likely see this trend expand to the point where whatever can be taught by computer, will be.

The modern computerized classroom bears little resemblance to the schoolroom of a few years ago where children chattered happily to each other between lessons, sitting two or four to a desk or table. The newest classrooms have each child at a terminal working on the programs for which he or she is responsible. This arrangement has the advantages of highly individualizing learning and of fitting curriculum to individual learning rates. Unfortunately, its greatest advantage is also its greatest disadvantage. Learning may become so individualized that the important socializing and humanizing aspects of the educative process are lost.

Some subjects, however, by their very nature, will never be taught by a computer program. Group singing still requires a group. A square dance still requires eight people. While some aspects of music can be (and are being) taught through computer programs, musical experience is still basically a social experience. To sing alone does not provide the pleasure that singing with another person or a whole choir does. Playing the cello or the trumpet is more fun in an ensemble or an orchestra. Music is both a socializing and a humanizing subject. Even people without a common language can communicate through music. Through music, people "speak to each other across time and beyond specific cultures."[7]

Music as a Spiritual and Uplifting Experience

Music has the capacity to touch people more deeply than mere words ever can. The aesthetic experience, for all that it is almost impossible to define, is nevertheless very real. Whether as audience members or as performers, people may be touched deeply by the Verdi Requiem, Puccini's *La Bohème*, Christmas carols sung by a

[6]Joan E. MacLeod, "Creative Potential and the Environment," *Fine* (Summer 1987), pp. 4–15.
[7]Ibid.

children's choir, the playing of the National Anthem, a favorite hymn, the soloist at a wedding, music played at a funeral. The music somehow helps lift the experience above the ordinary. Feelings normally inexpressible through language find expression in music. The emotional side is touched. Surely, the schools should nurture an art that has this capability.

CONCLUSION

At the dawn of the twenty-first century, music should occupy an important place in education. Whether such music education leads the student to a career in music, to music as a recreational activity, or to music simply as part of an audience, the contribution of music education to the fullest development of the capacities of the human mind, body, and emotions is unique. No other subject has as much potential to engage the total person or is so suited to a philosophy of holistic education.

CHAPTER 2

CREATING AN ENVIRONMENT FOR LEARNING MUSIC

Both physical setting and psychological surrounding must be considered in creating an effective environment in which children can learn music and, more important, will *want* to learn music. The former is fairly easy to design but somewhat less easy to achieve, since it demands planning and expenditure by the school system. The latter, the psychologically inviting setting, is dependent not upon budgets and books but upon the people involved in the educative process. If the psychological setting is a sound one, conducive to good teaching and learning, any deficiencies that may exist in the physical setting will be relatively unimportant to overall musical development.

THE PHYSICAL SETTING

The Classroom

The ideal room in which to teach music is a double-sized classroom with chairs and tables or desks at one end, facing a large chalkboard (staff-lined), and a large open space for movement at the other end. Along one wall there are enough bookcases to hold two or more class sets of music books, as well as a variety of supplementary music books, and along another are closed cabinets for storage of instruments, tapes, records, and discs. There are tables of the proper height for playing xylophones, resonator bells, and similar instruments. There are sturdy music stands. There is a *good* sound system with high-quality speakers. It is usable with records, tapes, and compact discs. A corner of the room has four or five individual tables with privacy screens. These tables have individual cassette tape decks and earphones for music listening and computers with a variety of musical games and programs in music. There is, of course, a piano, which is tuned regularly. There may be a set of electronic keyboards with earphones. There are windows along at least one wall for daylight and ventilation, and overhead lights that do not cause any glare on chalkboard or books.

This room does not exist in any school in which the author has ever taught, or even visited.

If a school *has* a music room, it usually has no furniture other than a piano (rarely in tune). The space is suitable for movement but terrible for singing. Children in such settings often have to sit (or sprawl) on the floor for singing. The posture necessary for good singing is simply impossible to achieve except by standing, and children cannot be expected to stand for the thirty to forty-five minutes of a music lesson.

It is far better in such situations to hold music lessons in the regular classroom setting. Although thirty or so desks occupy a great deal of space, it *is* possible to move them to the center quickly and efficiently and to use the space around them for movement, or to move them to the edges of the room and use the center space for movement. Such rearrangement of furniture can be routinized so that it takes a minimum of time and does not result in disorder or confusion. Books and instruments can be taken from room to room on a wheeled cart. The piano is not necessary for every lesson, but when it is needed it must be easily movable. Pianos set in a sort of cradle with large wheels are stable enough to be pushed from room to room. Small portable electronic pianos are also becoming an alternative for schools; they have the additional advantage that they hold their tuning.

Using the regular classroom for music teaching has a number of advantages. First, there are desks or tables and chairs. Second, this furniture is of the correct size for the children, which it seldom is in an "all-purpose" room. Third, time is not lost in moving children from one part of the building to another. Fourth, when the music lesson calls for pencil-and-paper work, the necessary tools are at hand and there is a surface on which each child can write. Fifth, the children can easily assume a good singing posture when sitting in correctly sized chairs (if the teacher reminds them to do so and shows them how). Sixth (and this is, perhaps, less obvious, but it is the most important), when music is taught in the same room as mathematics, science, and reading, there is an implication that it is a *subject* with a body of *knowledge* to be acquired, and not something to be equated with play period.

The one situation in which a separate room for music, however ill equipped, is preferable to the regular classroom is in "open-space" schools—schools without interior walls, in which three or four classes are conducted simultaneously by three or four teachers in one large open space. During the 1960s and 1970s, many new schools were constructed in this way. Today, few new schools are so designed, and increasing numbers of the older ones are putting up walls between the classes. The constant noise level of the "revolutionary" open-space school (a concept imported to North America from England) proved to be a deterrent to learning for many children and an inducer of nervous breakdowns and "burn-out" in teachers. Teachers assigned to such situations should take their music classes to any space they can find with walls and a door.

Using Spaces Other than the Classroom

The teacher should not overlook the possibilities of other spaces in the school for music instruction. Singing games and dances can be performed on the playground in good weather, or in the gym, the cafeteria, or a multipurpose room when those spaces are not in use by others.

Hallways are wonderful for singing games in facing line dance formation, and rounds sung in stairwells have a very special sound. Of course, care should be taken to ensure that moving the music class or a part of the music class to another place in the school building will not create problems for other classes and teachers.

The community, too, should be considered as a venue for the teaching of music. A fifth-grade class studying Bach should visit a local church with a good organ to see and hear live the kind of instrument for which Bach wrote so many compositions.

Trips to hear youth symphony concerts, opera for children, or folk music performers can enliven any instructional program in music. Further, such experiences tend to lead children to the conclusion that "school music" and "real music" are the same, not separate entities as they have occasionally been considered in the past.

THE PEOPLE

Many people potentially can be involved in music education in the schools: music teachers, supervisors and coordinators, classroom teachers, administrators, parents, and other members of the community. Too often, when responsibility is assigned to one of these, the others are ignored as resources. It is easy to think of music teaching solely as the province of the music teacher or coordinator. In actuality, the good music program is one that utilizes *all* the people who can make a contribution to musical learning. The trained music specialist does not have the advantage of the classroom teacher—that of being with the same children all day, five days a week. The classroom teacher rarely has the musical training or expertise to develop single-handedly a comprehensive program of musical instruction. Parents almost always want music for their children but are frequently unsure what form that instruction should take. Administrators generally schedule time for music in accordance with state or provincial guidelines, but they rarely have much to do with the teaching of music after scheduling it.

The classroom teacher who can bring all these disparate elements together to *contribute* to the music teaching in his or her class will have a rich and varied program.

The Roles of the Music Specialist and the Classroom Teacher

The music specialist has probably spent eight to twelve years studying an instrument and four to five years in courses such as music theory, history, form and analysis, music pedagogy, and music literature, in addition to those education courses needed for certification. As a result of such training, this person could be expected to assume principal responsibility for the music program in a school or schools, to act in an advisory capacity to classroom teachers in a number of schools, or to perform some combination of these two roles.

The music specialist who is expected to take full responsibility for the music program and is then given only one or two class periods a week in which to do so is in an untenable position. No one would expect the necessary skills for language, mathematics, or science to be developed in thirty minutes twice a week; yet, this is commonly expected of the music specialist-teacher. Such a teacher working cooperatively with classroom teachers can accomplish far more than he or she can accomplish working alone.

In such instances, the teacher-coordinator takes responsibility with the classroom teacher for the overall direction of the program—the setting of goals, the selection of teaching materials, and the development of teaching methods. The effectiveness of such a cooperative approach can be very great.

Other Human Resources

In some school systems, even today, there are no music specialists or coordinators at the elementary school level. Responsibility for music falls squarely on the classroom teacher. Most teachers are capable of giving children something in the way of a positive musical experience, but it should go without saying that some are more capable than others. The teacher who has not learned to carry a tune cannot very well teach singing, and the one who cannot keep a beat will not do very well teaching singing games and dances. In-service work may help, but a better and more efficient use of teacher time might be to poll the school to see who has musical training and would like to teach more music. In a school with eighteen teachers, there are probably three or four who are well able to teach music to two or three classes other than their own, and would enjoy doing so. This can be done in exchange for periods in physical education, art, second-language study, or almost any other subject in the curriculum for which the trading teacher has particular skills.

To the criticism that this leads to "departmentalization" and away from the "self-contained classroom," the only answer possible is that without a "self-contained *teacher*," there can certainly be no self-contained classroom, and the teacher has not yet been produced who is equally proficient at everything. All programs of instruction in an elementary school can benefit by the best utilization of individual teachers' talents and training.

When polling staff members to discover special abilities, teachers should not overlook administrators and parents. In one elementary school in which the author teaches, the principal has been a member of a folk club for years. When asked, he willingly brings his guitar into a classroom and sings with the children. The psychological impact of an authority figure—a man, at that—obviously valuing and enjoying music is immeasurable.

Parents, too, can bring richness and variety to the music program. A simple letter may be sent to all parents asking whether the parent (1) has ever been a music teacher; (2) is or has ever been a performer in a musical group; (3) plays any instrument and, if so, which; (4) would be willing to share his or her music with children. Such a letter must, of course, be approved by the school administration and would best be sent from the principal's office.

The responses can be very surprising. More than once, such a letter has netted a fully trained music teacher for the school, one who is "staying home with the children" but "wouldn't mind teaching a few classes on Tuesdays and Thursdays." Other times, a performer of professional level has emerged and has been delighted to demonstrate his or her instruments to classes. (On one such occasion, the author discovered a double-bass player with a major symphony orchestra among her kindergarten parents.) Accompanists for programs can also be found in this manner.

Failing to poll the school parent group for their musical interests can result in tremendous loss. In one instance of which the author has firsthand knowledge, a leading folk music performer and collector was never during the six years of his daughter's elementary school life invited to share his expertise with any class. He was listed on the usual school forms, correctly, as a professor of psychology, but no one ever bothered to find out that he was also one of the foremost scholars in North American folk music.

One school district in California tried an interesting experiment with parents.[1] When music and most other "special" subjects were eliminated from the curriculum in a tax-cutting spree, a grant was obtained to train parents with musical background to teach music as volunteers. The program was considered to be successful for a period of two years.

However, one point must be raised with regard to unpaid use of parents *instead* of teachers. To the extent that school systems "make do" with semiprofessional or volunteer help, they will be unable to show the need for professional help. While a volunteer approach is useful, even enriching to the curriculum on an occasional basis, if it becomes the *modus operandi* for a whole program, that program is doomed to extinction. No one is willing to volunteer forever. Professional work is deserving of a professional wage.

[1]Project Director: Nancy Kester, Alameda schools, 1979–80.

The line must be carefully drawn between using volunteers to enrich a program and expecting volunteer resources to become that program.

THE PSYCHOLOGICAL SURROUNDING

A caring teacher—one who enjoys working with children and who knows a repertory of twenty or thirty songs to sing with them—will probably do more for the music education of those children than the teacher who "knows all about music" and whose instruction is subject oriented rather than child centered. It is true that we cannot teach what we do not know, but the teacher who enjoys singing and who demonstrates that enjoyment by singing regularly with children will lead them to value music, while the more knowledgeable teacher teaching music "appreciation" may actually cause children to develop negative attitudes toward music. The difference is due to the ways in which children learn. It is related to the natural developmental stages through which children move in acquiring musical skills and inferring musical concepts.

Child Development

In the area of physical maturation, research has shown that the infant develops from the head downward and from the body center to the periphery.[2] Earliest physical responses are head movements. These are followed by sitting up, by standing, by using the hands to pick up objects, and, finally, by walking. The skill of walking is itself developmental. Infants' first secure steps must be on an even surface. Only later are they able to walk up and down stairs; later still, they learn to walk backwards and to run and climb. Much later, they can stand on one foot, briefly, and can gallop and jump.

The skills in the last group are not generally present before the end of the third year. Progress is irregular in motor skill development and may vary widely from child to child.

Piaget's Theory of Learning

There are many theories as to how children learn and what the various levels or stages of development are. Among the best known of these in twentieth-century education are those of Swiss psychologist Jean Piaget (1896–1980). He hypothesized that there are four different and distinct stages through which humans move in the acquisition of skills and knowledge.[3] The first of these he labeled the *sensorimotor period,* from birth to about two years of age. During this period, the child is concerned primarily with those things he or she can experience directly through the senses of seeing, hearing, smelling, tasting, and touching. Children in this stage know objects largely in terms of physical manipulation and develop motor memories based on sensory experiences; they begin to realize that certain behaviors produce certain predictable results.

The sensorimotor is a prelanguage level. It is a point of departure for all later perceptive and intellectual development; it begins at birth with the natural reflexes of suckling and grasping and ends when language and other symbolic ways of representing reality appear. The sensorimotor period is characterized by the gradual development of memory, by gradual changes in imitation and play, and by the appearance of first notions about space, time, and the causes of things.

[2]L. D. Crow and A. Crow, *Child Development and Adjustment* (New York: Macmillan, 1962).

[3]Jean Piaget and Bärbel Inhelder, *La Psychologie de l'enfant* (Paris: Presses Universitaires de France, 1966). Translated into English by Helen Weaver, *The Psychology of the Child* (New York: Basic Books, 1969).

At the beginning of the sensorimotor period, the child exists in a totally self-centered universe, but gradually in the first eighteen months of life, he or she moves to an awareness of self as an object among other objects.

The second stage, from about age two to age seven, Piaget refers to as *preoperational*. During this period, the child acquires language. He or she begins to be able to use symbols (aural-oral and visual) to represent objects. Symbolic play and imitation are the child's way of reacting to the world around him or her at this stage. Musically, singing games and chants are a natural part of this developmental stage.

Piaget characterizes the preoperational level as the time of "semiotic" or "symbolic" function. It is evidenced by the child's ability to evoke an object not present by

- Deferred imitation—the child crawling around in imitation of the dog when the dog is no longer in the room
- Symbolic play—the child playfully pretending to go to sleep
- Drawing—the child graphically representing his or her surroundings, particularly people
- Mental imagery—both evoking things seen previously and anticipating things not yet seen
- Verbal evocation—the child saying "meow" after the cat has gone

Imitation of the foregoing kinds is, according to Piaget, an "accommodation to external models," while play, on the other hand, "transforms reality by assimilation to the needs of the self."[4]

Intelligence, Piaget maintains, constitutes an equilibrium between such *assimilation* and *accommodation*.

Piaget describes four types of play:

1. *Exercise play.* This exists at the sensorimotor level and consists of repeating certain activities over and over again, such as batting at an object suspended over a crib.
2. *Symbolic play.* This is practiced between the ages of two and six. Rather than simply recalling events, the child re-creates them through play.
3. *Games with rules.* These games, typified by hopscotch, are the property of still older children and are transmitted socially from child to child.
4. *Games of construction.* These are games, initially symbolic, in which children work out solutions to problems.

Games provide a way for children to express life experiences, a way that is not dependent on language.

At the preoperational level, the child tends to reason through a process of *transduction;* that is, thought does not move from universal to particular (deduction) or from particular to universal (induction), but from particular to particular without generalization.

At the third stage, the *concrete operational* (ages about seven to eleven), the child is able to perceive and process more complex events, to find commonalities among diverse objects and events, and to classify and rank them. He or she is able to perceive the essential characteristics of an object or event, even if its context is changed. For example, in music, the child can identify which parts of a song are the same, which are different, and which are similar, and can use symbols to depict the forms of songs.

[4]Piaget and Inhelder, *La Psychologie de l'enfant*, p. 58.

Such activities are referred to as concrete operations because they relate to things seen, felt, or heard—to concrete realities rather than to verbally stated hypotheses. They act as a transition between actions and general logic.

In describing the difference between preoperational and concrete operational, Piaget uses the example of water transferred between two containers, the first short and fat, the second tall and thin. At four to six, the child will think there is more water in the tall glass, even after seeing it poured directly from the short one: The glass is taller; therefore, the water is more.

However, by seven or eight, the child will reason that since nothing has been added or taken away, the amount of water must be the same. This Piaget labels "*Simple or Additive Identities*." Further, a child at this level will suggest that if the water is put back in the short, fat glass, it will still be the same: the principle of "*Reversibility by Inversion*." Last, the child may reason that this is because the tall glass is narrower, while the short one is fatter: "*Compensation or Reversibility by Reciprocal Relationship*."

Concrete operations relate directly to objects, groups or classes of objects, counting of objects, and relationships between objects.

The egocentricity of the sensorimotor and preoperational levels is to a great extent replaced by cooperation with others during the period of concrete operations. Isolated play and play merely in the company of others largely disappear.

Children master several general groups of relationships during this period:

1. *Hierarchies of classes.* For example, they can understand that animals may be separated into

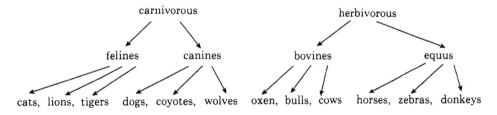

2. *Orders of succession.* They are able to line up with classmates in order of height or answer a roll call in alphabetic order.
3. *Substitution.* They discover different ways of achieving the end result—for example, in mathematics, knowing that 10 can be 9 + 1 or 8 + 2 or 6 + 4; in music, understanding that a measure of $\frac{4}{4}$ could be ♩ ♩ ♩ ♩ or ♩ ♩ or ○.
4. *Symmetrical relations.* They can understand that a distance is the same no matter in which direction one is going. For example, the distance from home to school is the same as the distance from school to home; if there are two brothers, each is a brother to the other. (This is a sharply different thinking level from the preconcrete, at which the child tends to exclude himself when recounting family relationships: *He* has a brother, but his brother has none, in his view.)
5. *Multiplication of classes.* Children can deal with double and even triple classifications, such as "Pick out all the *red squares*," or "Name a *pink flower* beginning with the letter *R*."
6. *Multiplication of series.* They are able to find a point on a map by using serial order of numbers in one direction and serial order of letters in the other.

In her book on Piaget and education, Beard makes the extremely valid point that much thinking at the junior high school stage is still proceeding at the intuitive level.[5] Students "know" multiplication or weight measurement tables but do not understand why they work. They may know and use key signatures but have no idea why these exist. There is danger if too much learning at this point is conducted verbally. There is still great need for a more hands-on problem-solving approach.

The last stage, the *formal or hypothetical operations* period (age eleven to adult), marks the beginning of abstract reasoning and the use of logic not specifically fastened to physical events or objects. Students at this stage are able to engage in quite complex musical analysis.[6]

At the formal operational stage, students are able to consider many viewpoints. They are more flexible in their thinking. They make decisions through discussion and reflection. Their moral judgments are less extreme; they no longer see the world as black and white.

Piaget theorized that around the age of twelve, children begin to be able to reason in propositions: "If such and such were to happen, then the result might be thus and so."

Some research has indicated that the capacity for thinking at this level does not develop before children are at a *mental* age of thirteen years.[7]

The implications for teaching in the elementary school are clear. Teaching should be in concrete terms. As Piaget says: "The essential difference between formal thought and concrete operations is that the latter are centered on reality, whereas the former grasps the possible transformations and assimilates reality only in terms of imagined or deduced events."[8]

According to Piaget, the thinking process from birth to adulthood moves

- From *concrete* to *abstract*
- From *immediate* to *remote*
- From *explicit* to *subtle*

Much of the research done since Piaget has borne out his theories.[9]

However, Piaget's "stages" should not be taken literally to mean that all children are at the same point at the same ages or that there is a sudden movement from one stage to the next at a specific age. There are five-year-olds operating at the concrete operational level and ten-year-olds operating at the preoperational level. It is demonstrably clear that children move through these stages on a sort of continuum rather than in finite steps, and, in addition, they move through them at different rates. Nevertheless, as an overall aid in knowing which kinds of experiences are most appropriate at which ages, the "stages" of Piaget are invaluable.

Bruner's Theory of Instruction

Jerome Bruner is an American psychologist whose ideas about teaching and learning have revolutionized thought regarding the instructional process.

While Piaget's ideas evolved into a "theory of learning"—an attempt to explain how learning takes place—Bruner's ideas form a "theory of instruction"—a

---

[5]Ruth M. Beard, *An Outline of Piaget's Developmental Psychology for Students and Teachers* (New York: Basic Books, 1969).

[6]Jean Sinor, "The Musical Development of Children and Its Application to the Kodály Pedagogy" (Oakland, Calif.: Organization of American Kodály Educators Conference, April 5-8, 1979).

[7]R. J. Mealings, "Problem-Solving in Science Teaching," *Educational Review*, xv (1963), 194–207; and E. A. Peel, *The Pupil's Thinking* (London: Oldbourne, 1960). See also Beard, *Piaget's Developmental Psychology*, p. 134 and Bibliography.

[8]Piaget and Inhelder, *La Psychologie de l'enfant*, p. 149.

[9]Herman T. Epstein and Marilyn P. Zimmerman, "State of the Art in Early Childhood Music and Research," in *The Young Child and Music: Contemporary Principles in Child Development and Music Education,* ed. Jacquelyn Boswell (Reston, Va.: Music Educators National Conference, 1985), pp. 65–78.

means to achieving *improvement* in learning. Where the former is descriptive, the latter is prescriptive. Piaget describes the observed stages through which humans progress in acquiring knowledge and skills. Bruner offers ways of achieving improvement in the acquisition of knowledge and skills.

Bruner said:

> Any idea or problem or body of knowledge can be presented in a form simple enough so that any particular learner can understand it in a recognizable form.[10]

In Bruner's theory, four aspects of instruction are considered:

- The predisposition of the learners
- The structure of the subject
- The sequence of presentation
- The means of reinforcing learning

The Predisposition of the Learners

Many factors influence the child to want to learn or not to want to learn about particular things long before he or she first comes to school. The home environment, the expressed likes and dislikes of parents and siblings, and early experiences outside the home may all influence a child's initial attitude toward learning and, thus, his or her ability to be taught effectively. Respect without fear for authority, possession of at least minimal social, language, and manipulative skills, and a predisposition to explore alternatives are all desirable entry-level behaviors for learning; they constitute a "predisposition to learn." Without them, the teaching-learning task is far more difficult.

Predisposition to learn in music will exist if the child comes from an environment that includes music. If the parents and siblings participate in musical activities, enjoy listening to music, and appear to value music, the child entering school will probably be predisposed to learn in the music class. If the home is without music or if music is considered to be unimportant, this will be reflected in the child's attitude, and the teaching-learning task will be considerably more difficult.

The Structure of the Subject

According to Bruner, the optimal structure of any subject matter is a small "set of propositions from which a larger body of knowledge can be generated."[11]

What Bruner calls "propositions" are what most educators refer to as "generalizations" or "underlying concepts."

If one thinks of this in terms of musical *form,* for example, all forms can be reduced to three basic propositions:

- Music has parts that are the same.
- Music has parts that are different.
- Music has parts that are similar.

(In similar parts, something is the *same* and something else is *different.*) The form of any music, from the smallest song to the longest symphony, may be analyzed in terms of these three basic "propositions."

Bruner's theory is based on providing learners with the broad structure of the subjects rather than with the mass of facts associated with those subjects.

---

[10]Jerome S. Bruner, *Toward a Theory of Instruction* (Cambridge: Harvard University Press, 1966), p. 44.

[11]Ibid., p. 41.

A concept or the connected body of concepts that is a theory is man's only means of getting a lot into the narrow compass of his attention all at a time. Without some such aid there is clutter.[12]

Bruner believed that a set of basic concepts had "generative" value; that is, they afforded the learners opportunity to go beyond facts and to generate new knowledge. His approach was what has become known as the *discovery process,* in which children use their existing knowledge and skills to uncover new knowledge.

Instruction consists of leading the learner through a sequence of statements and restatements of a problem or a body of knowledge that increases the learner's ability to grasp, transform, and transfer what he is learning.[13]

The Sequence of Presentation: Modes of Representation

According to Bruner, there are only three ways of encoding knowledge—only three "modes of representation": through action, through images, and through symbols.

While these are clearly stated from most to least concrete, Bruner see them as *emphases* in development rather than as stages in learning. Learners are expected eventually to master all three.

The first of these, referred to by Bruner as *enactive representation,* implies teaching-learning through actions things that are not easily taught through words. In music, for example, young children have great difficulty with "telling" what a beat is, but they have little difficulty demonstrating the beat by clapping or stepping it.

The second mode, named *iconic* by Bruner, involves using images or graphics to summarize or present a pictorial image of an experience without defining it fully. The child who pushes cutout felt shapes around on a felt board to demonstrate where the sounds are higher and where lower in the first phase of a song is engaged in this mode of representation. It is an inexact representation but a correct one—general contour notation rather than specific notation on a staff.

The third mode, *symbolic,* is the one most familiar in education. It is the world of *words* and *numbers,* and, in music, the world of traditional musical notation.

Bruner makes the point that it is important for teachers to recognize the mode through which learners are representing reality to themselves. The best sequence for teaching and learning, according to Bruner, is from enactive to iconic, and from iconic to symbolic—from experience gradually to the abstractions that represent that experience. If the enactive and iconic modes are bypassed in teaching, the learner may be unable to transfer knowledge from one situation to another. The specific symbols for one learning may actually interfere with accomplishing a related learning. The child who has stretched arms up high and dropped them toward the ground to illustrate higher and lower pitches in a song and who has pushed fuzzies around on a felt board to show where the sounds are higher and where lower will be able to do this for any interval or note grouping involving higher and lower pitches. To the contrary, the child who has worked only with staff notation and who knows how to notate a descending minor third from C to A has no tools for knowing how to encode an ascending fifth from E-flat to B-flat—or any interval other than the specific one(s) previously learned.

Reinforcing Learning

Bruner's theories about the teaching-learning task include ideas about how learning may be effectively reinforced. He suggests beginning learning in any sub-

---

[12]Jerome S. Bruner, *The Relevance of Education,* ed. Anita Gil (New York: W. W. Norton & Co., Inc., 1971), p. 123.

[13]Bruner, *Toward a Theory of Instruction,* p. 49.

ject area early and reinforcing learning through repeated revisitations over a number of years at increasingly more complex levels. It is his notion that any subject, reduced to its essential elements and major concepts, can be taught at any level.

Bruner's *Theory of Instruction* has had enormous influence in curriculum writing in the latter half of the twentieth century. Hardly a curriculum exists in which there has not been some attempt to focus on major concepts of a subject rather than on facts. The emphases in learning reinforcement and evaluation have shifted markedly from earlier models to ones in which learning is "revisited" and evaluation is related to the original goals and concepts.

Child Development in Music

The stages of development as outlined by Piaget and the instructional theory of Bruner have strong implications for music education. The most obvious conclusion is that earlier musical experiences must be concrete, immediate, and explicit and should be offered through the enactive stage; only later should music be dealt with as a symbolic language, abstract, remote, and subtle—the iconic and then the symbolic mode.

Psychologists tell us,

> If the play spirit prevails, the child is likely to persist until he attains successful achievement. He is then able to use his skill to enlarge his play activities. Thus play serves a useful purpose in the development of motor skills.[14]

Play does indeed serve a useful purpose in the development not only of motor skills but of all early musical skills.

In the first two years of life, the infant begins to move rhythmically and to use the voice to produce musical sounds. Infant babblings are themselves rhythmical, and as the young child develops the physical control of lip, tongue, and mouth muscles to begin producing bits of language, he or she also begins to produce bits of music. Gradually, these bits are expanded.

Among the most interesting studies on how children develop and learn musically is one done at Harvard University by Davidson, McKernon, and Gardner.[15] In this longevity study, Gardner and his associates examined the way in which children between birth and six years of age went about learning to sing. They made some useful comparisons between the stages in the acquisition of song and the developmental stages in the acquisition of language, mathematics, movement, and drawing skills. They found that by age one or one and a half, children generally produce their first two-word utterances, can distinguish between big and little seriated pieces, and can perform two different movements. Musically, they can sound their first discrete pitches by this age.

During the second year, children were observed to be able to repeat very short movement sequences, to reproduce events of two or three elements in story telling, and to produce first metaphors in language. In music, they could sing "repeatable characteristic bits" of melodies, could "recapture rhythm" of standard songs, and could demonstrate an approximation of pitch contour in songs with great contrast.

At three, children were able to draw simple objects recognizably and, in music, to reproduce a number of basic melodic fragments. By four, children used the words "and then" to string together unrelated events into "stories." Musically, for the first

---

[14]Crow and Crow, *Child Development and Adjustment,* p. 124.

[15]Lyle Davidson, Patricia McKernon, and Howard Gardner, "The Acquisition of Song: A Developmental Approach," in *National Symposium on the Applications of Psychology to the Teaching and Learning of Music,* Documentary Report of the Ann Arbor Symposium (Reston, Va.: Music Educators National Conference, 1981), pp. 301–15.

time, there appeared to be a sense of tonality within phrases. However, there was still no cross-phrase key stability. Only at five did key stability begin to emerge.

Dr. David Woods, Director of the School of Music of the University of Arizona, has described nine developmental stages and comprehension levels in music from the time the child enters school until he or she completes formal education.[16] The student:

LEVEL 1

Is able to discriminate, categorize, order, and rudimentally organize sound

Is in the early stages of conceptualizing rather than just perceiving sound and its parameters

Is beginning to read and to use language to describe social and physical reality

Has better control of large muscles than small ones

Does not yet have fully developed eye coordination and control

Often has difficulty matching pitch

Is developing a kinesthetic sense through an awareness of body position in space and through awareness of body movement alone and in relation to others

LEVEL 2

Is able to recall and to apply musical concepts

Is able to reorder musical ideas and is beginning to be able to improvise

Has better developed small muscles, and many parts of the body can be utilized in rhythmic activity

Thinks and reacts only in concrete terms

Has difficulty with abstractions

Has developed positive attitudes toward group activities and group involvement

Matches pitch somewhat more easily, and independent singing is being established

Is able to recognize some symbols and apply them to musical sounds

Can begin to read simplified forms of music notation as a part of the learning process

LEVEL 3

Learns best through activity

Has better-developed finger and hand coordination for musical tasks

Is able to accept a variety of new musical concepts and to apply them in creative activities, including improvisation and composition

Is beginning to be able to read music and sing harmony parts

Is achieving personal independence in music and is able to use logical operations such as reversibility, classification, and serialization

LEVEL 4

Is beginning to think abstractly

Is able to create music using more complex musical forms

Is able to identify major and minor modes, certain intervals, and various timbres, dynamic levels, tempos, and styles

[16]Stefan Edelstein, Lois Choksy, Paul Lehman, Njotll Sigurdson, and David Woods, *Creating Curriculum in Music* (Reading, Mass.: Addison-Wesley, 1980).

Is beginning to develop a set of social values

Is able to reason and to solve musical problems

Reads music and is able to sing and play classroom instruments independently

LEVEL 5

Has a high capacity for work, and success is extremely important

Has achieved certain instrumental and vocal skills

Is able to organize sounds using many musical forms

Is beginning to understand the scientific principles of sound production and reproduction

Is able to apply these principles and concepts when writing for special timbres

LEVEL 6

Improvises freely and easily

Has had experience playing and writing for all the classroom instruments

Is able to use technical vocabulary in analyzing and describing music

Has developed vocal independence and a high level of proficiency in sight reading

Is able to sing and to play some of the standard repertoire for ensembles

LEVEL 7

Has achieved a high level of abstract thinking ability and is capable of examining and testing hypotheses

Is able to experiment with musical forms

Is working toward a high level of vocal and/or instrumental proficiency and is able independently to prepare and perform works from the standard repertoire

Has been exposed to many types of music and is able to analyze the forms and styles utilized

Is able to compose with ease in many musical styles

Is able to make musical evaluations based on a comprehensive understanding of music

LEVEL 8

Has acquired a highly sophisticated set of musical values and standards

Has further developed personal performance skills and abilities

Is able to demonstrate a variety of styles and techniques in performance and composition and is able to analyze and describe these techniques

Has developed musical independence and can make decisions in music which reflect personal taste

LEVEL 9

Has achieved high musical standards in personal performance

Understands the technical and the theoretical aspects of music and is knowledgeable with respect to the historical development of music

Is able to discuss intelligently a variety of topics regarding music and musicians

Is able to criticize performances, including his or her own, and to make or suggest desirable changes

Has in essence become a comprehensive musician

It is important to recognize that these "levels" are *not* grades and that they relate to age in only a general way. There may be nine- or ten-year-olds operating at Level 2, while others of the same age, perhaps musically gifted, could be operating at Level 9. What this organization into levels does offer the teacher is an understanding of the stages through which the child must progress to achieve his or her fullest musical potential.

CONCLUSION

A good music program is dependent upon adequate and suitable music space, trained and competent teachers and other associated personnel, and an understanding of how children learn in music. However, given the latter two, any lack in the first will be relatively unimportant to children's musical development.

CHAPTER 3

ACTIVITIES THROUGH WHICH CHILDREN LEARN MUSIC
Singing

Most children engage in some form of spontaneous singing when left to their own devices. Often, with the youngest children, this singing takes the form of a single musical pattern sung over and over again in a soft, plaintive tone. Children may sing to themselves while playing with a favorite toy, or they may lull themselves to sleep with such singsong chants at naptime. This singing is neither organized nor communal. For the youngest children, singing is a solitary activity, something they do to please themselves. It is as natural an expression to them as speaking, and indeed, few young children actually perceive the difference between singing and speaking. They move freely from one to the other.

When children come to the nursery school or kindergarten, they are thrust suddenly into an environment in which they are expected to sing with others and to sing tunes determined by their teacher, at times established by the teacher, and they are even asked by some teachers not to hum or sing to themselves while they do their other school tasks. Formal "songs" replace their previous musical meanderings.

CHILDREN'S ACQUISITION OF SONG

Children's acquisition of song is in itself an interesting phenomenon, the subject of research and writing. There is considerable agreement in the literature that the first intervals to be sung accurately in the context of melodies are seconds and thirds, and that these are followed by perfect fourths and fifths. Davidson[1] refers to these as "contour schemes" of a third, fourth, and fifth rather than as intervals, and goes on to report that young children's high-low motion of a third is followed later by a filling-in of the third, with the note between producing two seconds, which is followed still later by a leap involving the fourth.

Example 1 shows the relative pitches of the common young children's chant,

---

[1]Lyle Davidson, "Preschool Children's Tonal Knowledge: Antecedents of Scale," in *The Young Child and Music: Contemporary Principles in Child Development and Music Education,* ed. Jacquelyn Boswell (Reston, Va.: Music Educators National Conference, 1985), pp. 25–40.

21

EXAMPLE 1

which has been referred to by conductor Leonard Bernstein as "a joint product of our human genetic predisposition and the physical laws that govern musical harmony. . . . These three universal notes [la-so-mi] are handed to us on a silver platter."[2]

There are, of course, divergent views to this one so eloquently expressed by Bernstein. Some music educators feel that this so-called universal three-note chant is in reality only a result of the harmonic system favored by the western world, that it is a part of our culture, and that in singing these tones, children simply reflect the society in which they live.

Whichever theory is correct, whether there is a "universal infant song" or whether the earliest melodies of young children are a reflection of the surrounding culture and language, it is a fact that children do both sing old chants on these three relative pitches (Example 2) and improvise new texts to them (Example 3).

EXAMPLE 2

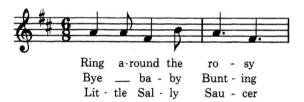

Ring   a-round the   ro - sy
Bye __ ba - by   Bunt - ing
Lit - tle Sal - ly   Sau - cer

EXAMPLE 3

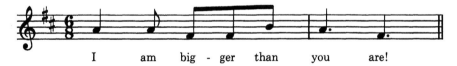

I   am   big - ger   than   you   are!

A reality is that there are too many early childhood chants and singing games built on these tones to be dismissed as pure chance. One may hear them on any playground. Because they are common to English-speaking children, they are a logical place to begin the instruction of singing in the classroom.

Songs based on this early childhood chant, such as "Ring around the Rosy," "Little Sally Saucer," and "Bye Baby Bunting," are known by many children when they come to school, and their melodic and rhythmic simplicity and repetitive texts cause them to be easily acquired by those children who don't already know them.

The teacher can use these notes also in his or her morning greeting to the class (Example 4) and to individuals (Example 5) or to solicit musical responses from children (Example 6).

However, a diet of songs built on only these three tones would be boring, indeed, and, worse than boring, could have the deleterious effect of curtailing children's natural musical development rather than enhancing it. The simple three-note chants of early childhood should be used, but they must be supplemented by songs of wider range and more complex rhythms or children will become musically

[2]Howard Gardner, "Do Babies Sing a Universal Song?" *Psychology Today,* 15, no. 12 (1981), 76–77.

EXAMPLE 4

Good   morn - ing,   boys   and   girls!

EXAMPLE 5

Good   morn - ing,   Su - san

EXAMPLE 6

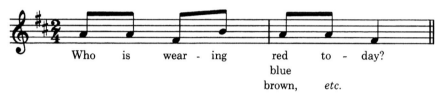

Who   is   wear - ing   red   to - day?
                         blue
                         brown,   *etc.*

What   did   you   have   for   break - fast?

stunted. (Think what the effect on children's acquisition of language would be if adults spoke to children using only the words in a four-year-old's vocabulary.)

Children do not learn these more complex songs as quickly or as easily as they do the chants.

According to Davidson, McKernon, and Gardner, five-year-old children go through essentially four stages in the acquisition of a song.[3]

Phase 1—TOPOLOGY

The underlying beat is present in the children's singing.

The tempo is established.

The words of the whole song or of the most distinctive phrases are acquired.

The number and the order of phrases are correct. (This is supported largely by the framework of the words.)

Phase 2—RHYTHMIC SURFACE

The child can reproduce the rhythm of a song exactly (note-for-note on a drum, for example) and can synchronize it with the underlying beat.

The child sings an approximation of the pitch contours of the most distinctive phrases but maintains no key stability across phrases. Intervals vary from one rendition to the next.

[3]Lyle Davidson, Patricia McKernon, and Howard Gardner, "The Acquisition of Song: A Developmental Approach," in *National Symposium on the Applications of Psychology to the Teaching and Learning of Music,* Documentary Report of the Ann Arbor Symposium (Reston, Va.: Music Educators National Conference, 1981), pp. 301–15.

Phase 3—PITCH CONTOUR

The child attempts to match pitch contour for each phrase, but cross-phrase key stability is still absent.

Intervals still vary from one singing of the song to the next.

Phase 4—KEY STABILITY

There is a clear projection of tonality across phrases, although intervals within phrases are still not always correct.

The child can extract the underlying beat from surface rhythms.

The child exhibits an ability to perform expressive transformations (for example, to sing at a slower tempo for a sad verse of the song).

In these research findings, there are implications for teaching songs to children. First, it is clear that children need to hear a song correctly performed many times if they are to reproduce it correctly. The idea that a new song may be "taught" to five- or six-year-olds as a part of one singing period is obviously not based in reality. Rather, the teaching, like the learning, should be thought of as a several-staged process.

At the first introduction of the new song, there should be no attempt to have the children sing it. Rather, the experience should be one in focused listening. The teacher should sing the song as musically and expressively as possible, in the tempo at which the children will later be expected to perform it. He or she should then guide the children to discuss the text and meaning of the song. The teacher can sing it again to have children discover aspects of the text they missed or to confirm their findings.

This sort of "listening" and "discussion" can be repeated several times over a number of days. Just as young children want to hear favorite stories over and over again, they enjoy hearing songs repeatedly.

In the later listenings, children will begin spontaneously to "sing along" on characteristic bits of the song, on repeated words or phrases:

"The town-o, the town-o, the town-o!"
"Here, Blue! You good dog, you!"

When they can do this, the teacher may have them attempt to sing along through the entire song. Pitch may be only approximate, but children can probably now keep the beat or tap the rhythm while singing. The teacher should continue to model correct melody.

When beat and rhythm are established, time should be spent focusing on correcting melodic problems. Some parts of the song may need to be isolated and practiced. Children should be given opportunity to sing the song or parts of the song both in the group and individually. Dynamic and tempo variations, if any, may be discussed and implemented.

Throughout the process, it is essential that the teacher maintain a mental attitude of "teaching." Too often, a song is presented once, learned inaccurately, sung incorrectly, and then forever after performed that way by a class. By thinking of the teaching of a song as a long-range rather than a single-lesson strategy, the teacher is more likely to achieve a genuinely musical result.

To summarize, the steps in presentation of a new song might be these:

THE TEACHER	THE CHILDREN
1. Sings the song expressively with attention to phrasing, dynamics, tempo, and text.	1. Listen to the song.

THE TEACHER *(cont.)*

2. Asks guide questions to focus attention on "what happens" in the song. Sings again as necessary for correct answers.

3. Sings the whole song; indicates with a motion where children are to "join in." Shows melodic contour with hand levels for the parts the children sing.

4. Sings the whole song. Demonstrates the beat while singing by conducting or tapping.

5. Sings the song phrasewise, showing melodic contour by hand levels.

6. Asks questions that will lead to more expressive singing through the use of dynamics and tempo.

THE CHILDREN *(cont.)*

2. Focus on text and meaning. Discover the "order of events" in the song.

3. Sing characteristic repeated parts of the song with the teacher.

4. Sing the whole song. Tap the beat. Clap the rhythm.

5. Work on correcting any melodic problems, repeating the song phrasewise after the teacher.

6. Use dynamics and tempo to underline the meaning of the text and the character of the music.

These six steps could take two lessons or six lessons or even more with younger children. There is no absolute time line for moving through them. However, to skip a step is to make song acquisition more difficult.

While the preceding process is intended primarily for use with five- and six-year-olds, the approach to a new rote song through first listening to it over two or three lessons is effective even with fifth and sixth graders, particularly when the melody is unusual, perhaps in an unfamiliar mode, and text is involved. Older children learn a song they have heard a few times more quickly and accurately than one that is brand new to them.

All of the foregoing is based upon the premise that singing will be unaccompanied. The best model for a voice is a voice. The teacher who is presenting a new song from the keyboard is usually blissfully unaware of the sounds being produced by the children. And these sounds usually bear little relationship to the actual melody of the song. Harmonics blur the melody line, and a piano accompaniment, at even a moderate dynamic level, tends to cause young voices to sing more heavily than they should. The teacher who is unsure vocally would do better to play melodies on recorder, resonator bells, or xylophone, rather than piano.

When a piece is known well and is being sung accurately, a light accompaniment may be added if desired. However, the piano is addictive both for children and for teacher. It is easy to become dependent upon it. It requires far less thought and energy on the part of both the teacher and the children to "sing along" with a piano than it does to focus on the vocal sounds being produced.

CHILDREN'S VOCAL RANGE

There have been many studies of young vocal range. However, the contradictions in much of this research are so rampant that one is left wondering of what value any of it is. Conflicting reports variously give the range of five-year-old children as shown in Example 7. The problem with most of these studies is that they depict the extreme ranges at which children can produce any recognizable pitch rather than the ranges in which young children naturally sing songs.

EXAMPLE 7

EXAMPLE 7 *(cont.)*

It has been the author's experience that most young children have a fairly limited range within which they can correctly reproduce melodies using a head tone, and that that range generally lies between D and A or B-flat (Example 8). There is for most five- or six-year-olds a distinct break in the voice around middle C where the voice moves from a head to a chest tone.

EXAMPLE 8

In research, the distinction has not usually been made between correctly produced vocal sounds—the "head voice," in which children should be singing if vocal damage is not to result—and "chest voice" pitches.

It is probably no accident that earlier studies indicate fewer pitches in the chest range. In earlier days, the models for children's singing were mothers', classmates', and teachers' voices. Today, more often than not, the models are radio, television, and recordings. Popular performers in these media almost always produce harsh chest tones, which are further exaggerated by amplification. Little wonder that children come to school singing F below middle C in voices that sound thirty years old.

It is vitally important that when considering range, the teacher consider only the range in which the child can accurately produce a head tone—the range in which songs can be comfortably sung. It is this author's belief that that has not changed significantly since 1895, when Paulsen found it to be D to A (Example 9).

EXAMPLE 9

VOCAL QUALITY

Children should be encouraged to sing in light but energetic, not listless, voices, and with a simple natural vocal quality. They should be taught to breathe at ends of phrases rather than in the middle of phrases or words, and to sing on vowels or the stressed vowel of diphthongs rather than on consonants or the so-called vanishing vowel of the diphthong as is so often done in popular music.

In English pronunciation, diphthongs are common:

"a" as in day is actually made up of two vowel sounds, *a* and *ee*

"i" as in night is *i—ee*

"o" as in snow is *o—oo*

"ou" as in hour is *ah—oo*

"oy" as in joy is *o—ee*

Children should sing on the first sound of each of these diphthongs and let the second one "disappear."

Some diphthongs require sustaining the second of the two sounds, moving quickly through the first:

"ew" as in dew is *ee—oo* (sung on the *oo* sound)

With older children it is possible to discuss these techniques that lead to more beautiful singing, but with younger ones, good vocal techniques and enunciation should simply be modeled in the teacher's singing. Children are natural mimics. What the teacher does, they will imitate.

Sometimes, a teacher feels unable to sing in the correct range and with the vocal quality needed for modeling singing for children. Adults, too, have had before them, for most of their lives, the example of the pop music chest voice. For them, too, this is sometimes the vocal quality easiest to imitate. There is a fear of the upper ranges and head tones, as there tends to be fear of anything unknown and untried. However, in twenty years of training teachers, the author has never known one woman who could not, with help, learn to sing in the range best for children's voices. The solution is to sing softly and lightly with a childlike tone, in a sort of half voice.

Men, of course, face a different sort of problem in that their natural voices usually sound an octave below children's. It is not uncommon for children to attempt to match exactly the pitch a male teacher is singing. They should be gently discouraged from doing this. If the male teacher can produce a good falsetto sound, he may demonstrate to children where their voices should be placed and have them focus on the two sounds, theirs and his. If falsetto is difficult for the male teacher, a child who sings accurately and with correct placement may be used as the "example" for the class.

On no account should the male teacher simply sing continuously in falsetto with his children. Such a use of the voice can lead to vocal cord damage and is, in any case, unnecessary. Children do adjust quickly to the male voice.

HELPING THE OUT-OF-TUNE SINGER

To a certain extent, in-tune singing is a matter of maturation. If singing is a daily class activity, most children will sing in tune by the end of second grade. However, there are techniques that may speed this process up and that could also prove useful for the children who appear still to be having trouble "finding their singing voices" after grade two.[4]

The phrase "finding the singing voice" is psychologically an important one for both the teacher and the children. The attitude must be that "everyone has one" and that we simply have to "find yours." Everything the teacher does to help the child with pitch problems must be thought of and expressed in these positive terms. Never should such a child be asked to sit mutely while others sing unless there is a physical problem with the voice that has be diagnosed by a doctor.[5]

Some factors that can influence children's ability to sing in tune are

- A home environment without music
- A psychological problem—for example, having been told by parent(s), siblings, or friends that "you can't sing"
- A physical problem—hearing loss or vocal cord damage

[4]For a study of one effective process, see Elizabeth Fleming, "Developing Melodic Singing Accuracy in Grade One Students" (M. Mus. Thesis, The University of Calgary, 1989).

[5]It is a sad fact that an increasing number of children have vocal cord damage. Problems are evidenced by hoarse speech, an extremely limited singing range, and a hazy singing quality. Such children should be referred to speech therapists if the school district has them, and parents should be made aware of the possibility of vocal cord damage.

Only the last of these cannot be counteracted in the classroom.

The most important step for the teacher to take in helping children acquire accurate pitch is the establishment of a safe and supportive musical environment. Ridicule or laughter by other children at a child's singing attempts must be strictly forbidden. Rather, an atmosphere in which children applaud each other's attempts is to be fostered. The teacher, too, can contribute to the security of the vocally shy child by holding his or her hands, establishing eye contact, and singing softly along with him or her. The eye contact tends to close out the rest of the world for the child, and the support of the teacher's voice makes singing "alone" easier. Of course, children must sing alone if they are to be helped vocally. Classes do not have pitch problems; individuals have them, and solutions must suit individual problems.

SOME PITCH PROBLEMS AND POSSIBLE SOLUTIONS

Speech-Pitched or Dronelike Singing

The child with this problem usually has not distinguished between speaking and singing. Activities that aid in developing this kind of discrimination are necessary (see Example 10). If the child continues to speak the singing phrase, ask him or her, "Was that your speaking voice or your singing voice?" If he or she is uncertain, the teacher must say, "It was your speaking voice." Unless children know whether or not they have achieved what is asked for, they have no idea what they should be working toward. The child who knows he or she is speaking rather than singing will listen more closely to the singing phrase and will try harder to imitate the sounds. It is occasionally helpful to have a child place hands on the teacher's throat and then on his or her own during this speaking and singing exercise. The quality of the vibrations is noticeably more regular during singing.

EXAMPLE 10

When the child finally produces the phrase in a singing sound, at any pitch, there should be general rejoicing. He or she should be given the feeling of accomplishment. Praise is a wonderful motivator, and it takes only a moment of the teacher's time.

Singing Intervals and Melodic Patterns
More or Less Correctly but at a Pitch Lower
than That of the Class

This is a more common problem than the speech-pitched drone, and it is also usually the next stage for the child moving from the speech-pitched drone toward in-tune singing. Children who sing in correct rhythm and with approximately correct tune, but at an appreciably lower pitch than the rest of the class, have not "found" their head voices. They are singing in chest voices. The voice placement is incorrect and potentially damaging to the child voice.

Two techniques have proven helpful to the author with such singers. The first and simpler is to take the head voice out of the musical context and make of it a gamelike activity:

Engine, Engine Number Nine,
Going down Chicago Line,
If the train goes off the track
Do I get my money back?

The class chugs around the room being a train. At the end of the song, the engine whistle must blow:

oo - oo - oo

Various children take turns singing the part of the train whistle. The teacher should initially pick children who will be sure to sing it accurately. After several children with clear head voice have done the "whistle," one of the children who has been unable to produce a head-voiced pitch should be given the opportunity. It is amazing how many who "can't sing high" can be a high train whistle. They don't consider that "singing."

Of course, for this technique to be effective, transfer must be made from train whistle to song:

"John, do the train whistle. . . . Good! Now do the train whistle again, and then sing "Rain, Rain, Go Away" on the train whistle sounds."

It may be necessary for a few weeks to help John begin every song by first "doing the train whistle," but eventually singing in a head voice will become natural to him.

A second technique for moving the child voice from chest to head placement is based on findings of the French hearing specialist A. A. Tomatis, who has spent a lifetime investigating musical hearing and its effect on vocal production. Tomatis found the right ear to be the ear of intervallic identification. The author has transferred his findings into classroom practice by walking around the room singing as the class sings, and periodically leaning over to sing a phrase or two into a child's right ear. Sometimes nothing happens. At other times the result is phenomenal. The voice of the child being so treated slides up to precisely the pitch of the teacher and follows the teacher's voice accurately note-by-note as long as the teacher continues to sing in the child's right ear. When the teacher moves away, the child's voice almost invariably slips back to its chest placement.

The value of this exercise is that the teacher knows now that the child can sing in a head tone. It is important to repeat the exercise without the rest of the class singing so that the child can be made aware of what he or she is doing. Again, praise will help reinforce the behavior:

"Listen to Jane's high voice! Isn't it beautiful!"

When children are first learning to use head voices, they often slip back into earlier modes of singing. It requires great effort and concentration initially to sing in the "new voice." Regular encouragement is needed.

"Wandering" Pitch

Sometimes children sing in lovely head tones, but the pitches they sing bear little resemblance to the melody of the song being sung by the class. The pitches just seem to wander. Of all pitch problems, this is the one most needing individual help outside regular class time. Often, the child with such a problem is unfocused in many subjects, not just in music, and it is this lack of concentration that causes pitch to wander.

In attempting to help such a child, choose musical materials with simple rhythms and of small melodic range. Working individually with him or her, sing in a slow tempo, using songs he or she knows extremely thoroughly. Be particularly careful that his or her starting pitch is exactly as you give it. Work for only brief periods with the child, but do so as frequently as time will allow. Above all, help the child to identify when he or she is singing correctly and when incorrectly. This requires great tact on the part of the teacher so that the child will want to continue to try. Fortunately, this kind of vocal problem is relatively rare. Most out-of-tune singers fall into one of the first two types discussed here.

Some other considerations in helping children with pitch problems are these:

1. Children will sing a tune they know very well more accurately than one they learned just last week. While that might seem obvious, it bears remembering. Familiarity with the music aids in-tune singing. Use the best-known songs for working with pitch problems.

2. Singing depends upon first hearing and then inner-hearing the pitch or melodic line to be reproduced. It is not possible to sing a sound without first "thinking" or "imagining" that sound. Children need time to focus their inner hearing on what is to be sung.

3. The teacher must use consistent and accurate pitch terminology if children are to understand what is being asked of them. *Up* and *down* are words of direction, not of pitch. "Can you make your voice match mine?" or "Can you sing that in a higher place?" is more likely to result in a higher singing pitch than "Can you make your voice go up?"

CLASS SINGING

While some individual singing should be done as part of each music class, most singing will be done by the whole class. How does one get thirty or so children to start a song, all on the same pitch, in the same tempo, and at the same time?

First, the teacher must have a tonality and a starting pitch in his or her own mind. If the teacher is working from printed music and that music is in a key suitable for children's singing, the task is easier. Look at the last note of the song and the key signature to find the "keynote" (*do* in major, *la* in minor).[6]

If able, the teacher may use an A440 tuning fork to find the keynote. Otherwise, he or she may find this note on the keyboard or the resonator bells. If sense of key is secure, he or she should look at the starting note of the song and find it in relation to the keynote. The musically less secure teacher can, in addition, play a tonic chord 1-3-5 on the keyboard or resonator bells to establish the tonality. Next, the teacher sings the first phrase silently, thinking through the tune and deciding on the tempo (speed of the beat).

It takes far longer to write or read the foregoing than actually to do it. In writing lesson plans, the teacher should write the keynote (F, for example) beside the song title, as well as the starting pitch (A, *mi*, for example).

[6]See Chapter 10, pp. 125–28, for a detailed discussion on key signatures.

Once the teacher has tonality, starting pitch, and tempo in mind, he or she sings the first phrase of the song to the children so that they will have the tonality and the tempo in mind. Then, *on the starting pitch,* the teacher sings "1, 2, Ready, Sing" or some such guide so that all will start together. This lead-in to singing must be in the tempo and meter of the song. For $\frac{2}{4}$ or $\frac{4}{4}$ songs it might be

while for $\frac{6}{8}$ it could be:

or for triple meter:

A song beginning with an upbeat must use the section missing from the opening bar as its lead-in. "Happy Birthday," for example, begins with a two-eighth-note upbeat. For this, the rhythm of the last two bars of the song should be used to get children started:

To help the music flow smoothly once started, the teacher may perform simple conducting gestures throughout.[7]

Singing in Parts

If children have learned to sing in tune in grades one and two and have acquired a repertory of rote songs, they should be able to sing easy two-part arrangements in grades three and four. The simplest of these are ostinati, canons, and descants, and the easiest way to begin two-voice singing is by adding a second part to a song already well known.

For example, to the song "Rain, Come Wet Me" (Example 11) add an ostinato (Example 12).

EXAMPLE 11

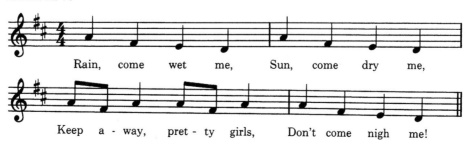

[7]See Chapter 9, pp. 100–102.

EXAMPLE 12

Rain, rain, go a - way.

With the song "Hey, Betty Martin," a simple descant or countermelody adds interest (Example 13).

EXAMPLE 13

Tip - toe, Hey, Bet - ty Mar - tin,

Hey, Bet - ty Mar - tin, Tip - toe, tip - toe;

Tip - toe, tip - toe fine; Tip - toe,

Hey, Bet-ty Mar - tin, tip - toe fine; Hey, Bet-ty Mar-tin,

Hey, Bet-ty Mar - tin, Tip - toe, Please be mine!

Tip - toe, tip - toe; Hey, Bet-ty Mar - tin, Please be mine!

Every child has sung the rounds "Brother John" and "Row Your Boat." Other rounds and canons should be added and a repertory of these developed. To teach any second part, whether ostinato, descant, or canon, the teacher must know it extremely securely first. Follow this procedure to teach a second part:

1. The children sing the original song softly while the teacher sings the second part. This should be done several times, until the children are able to maintain "their part" while hearing "the teacher's part."

2. The teacher teaches the second part by rote as he or she would teach any rote song, working out any rhythmic difficulties with the children and using hand levels to indicate melodic contour.

3. When the second part seems secure, the teacher sings the original song while the children sing the second part. This is also practiced until secure.

4. The class is divided into two sections. Half sing the original melody while the other half sing the new part. The two sections then reverse parts.

This sequence of steps is designed to develop independence in part singing. It does not require or depend upon strong "leaders" for the parts but, rather, ensures that all children know all parts well.

In fifth and sixth grades, part singing should be expanded to include more involved descants, canons at intervals other than unison, and simple two- and three-part harmonic arrangements.[8]

CONCLUSION

Singing is fundamental to all musical learning. The voice is an instrument every person has from birth, and to use that instrument for singing is as natural an activity as to use it for speaking.

Children love to sing. Even those unfortunate older students without musical experience who profess to "hate music" are in reality only expressing fear—a fear that can be overcome through singing.

The teacher who sings regularly with his or her children is presenting them with a gift that will provide them with lifelong enjoyment. Even if nothing else is accomplished in the music class, the time will not have been wasted.

ACTIVITIES

1. Choose a song from a series book. Prepare it and teach it to your class by rote, following the suggestions on pages 24 and 25.

2. Choose and teach to your classmates a canon or song with ostinato or descant, following the teaching order given on pages 32 and 33.

3. Use series books and other sources (see the following suggestions) to make a list of
   a. Patriotic songs every child should know
   b. Folksongs every child should know
   c. Rounds and canons for assembly singing

4. Choose a core of songs that may help with developing in-tune singing. Tell why each is good and how to use it.

SOME SUGGESTED SOURCES FOR SONGS

1. RICHARD JOHNSTON, *Folk Songs North America Sings.* Toronto: E. C. Kerby Ltd., 1984.
2. EDITH FOWKE, *The Penguin Book of Canadian Folk Songs.* Markham, Ont.: Penguin Books Canada Ltd., 1986.
3. ALAN LOMAX, *The Folk Songs of North America.* Garden City, N.Y.: Doubleday, 1960.
4. JOHN LOMAX, ALAN LOMAX, and RUTH CRAWFORD SEEGER, *Folk Song U.S.A.* New York: NAL, 1941.
5. EDITH FOWKE, *Sally Go Round the Sun.* Garden City, N.Y.: Doubleday, 1969.
6. EDITH FOWKE, *Ring around the Moon.* Englewood Cliffs, N. J.: Prentice-Hall, 1977.
7. RUTH CRAWFORD SEEGER, *American Folk Songs for Children,* Garden City, N.Y.: Doubleday, 1948
8. PETER ERDEI and KATALIN KOMLOS, *150 American Folk Songs to Sing and Play.* New York: Boosey & Hawkes, Inc., 1974.
9. ELEANOR LOCKE, *Sail Away.* New York: Boosey & Hawkes, Inc., 1988.

[8]See *Music for Children's Choirs: A Selective and Graded Listing.* Donald W. Roach, Project Coordinator (Reston, Va.: Music Educators National Conference, 1977).

CHAPTER 4

ACTIVITIES THROUGH WHICH CHILDREN LEARN MUSIC
Moving

Children do not perceive singing and moving to music as different activities but as two parts of the same activity, each dependent upon the other. They may have difficulty singing the words to a game song when sitting down, but they have *no* difficulty when playing the game. The movements call to mind the words and melody of the game. Any song with associated motions is easier for young children to learn and to retain than a song without movement. Movement to music contributes to the development of body control, offers stimulus to children's imaginations, provides them with an emotional outlet, and encourages a willingness to experiment. Movement has the added advantage that it is the most easily accessible and teachable aspect of music for the classroom teacher. No special skill beyond ability to maintain a steady beat is necessary to bring the joy of movement to children.

Three types of movement will be considered in this chapter:

- Movement to traditional singing games and dances
- Creative movement
- Movement for specific teaching purposes

MOVEMENT TO TRADITIONAL SINGING GAMES AND DANCES

The old games shown in Examples 1 and 2, and others like them, have been sung and played by generations of North American children.[1]

While some of these will survive whether or not the school takes a hand, the relative isolation of children in today's society could herald the disappearance of many.

Children today rarely play together after school and on weekends as they did a few decades ago. Today, their lives are filled with organized activities—piano or ballet lessons, Little League, Scouts, and so on. Such time as is not organized in that

[1]For a comprehensive guide to the games and dances of North American children, see Lois Choksy and David Brummitt, *120 Singing Games and Dances* (Englewood Cliffs, N. J.: Prentice-Hall, 1987).

EXAMPLE 1 "London Bridge Is Falling Down"

EXAMPLE 2 "Here We Go 'round the Mulberry Bush"

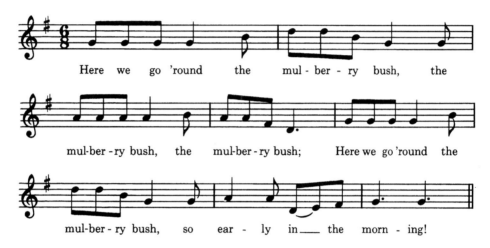

fashion tends to be spent in front of the television or with that newest inducer of isolation—the household computer.

Although some of these substitutes for the older forms of children's play have worth, it would nevertheless be a pity to lose the wonderful tradition of children's singing games and dances, with its humanizing and socializing values. The school can and should provide a place for this heritage.

Singing games and dances may be roughly divided into those of young children, which are more gamelike in character, and those for older youngsters, which are more dancelike.

Singing Games

The circle is the most common formation found in young children's games, and the simplest type of game is the one in which one child in the center of the circle acts out what the words describe (Example 3). Games of this type abound in the literature and are highly suitable for five- to seven-year-olds.

Other types of early childhood circle games involve partner-choosing (Example 4) and chasing each other around the outside of the circle (Example 5).

In addition to circle games, there are games involving "follow the leader" (Example 6), lines with bridges or arches that sometimes "fall" on the passers-through (Example 7), and confrontation between facing lines (Example 8).

All these are a part of the tradition of North American children and, more important, can provide endless hours of entertainment and fun for the kindergarten or first- or second-grade child.

EXAMPLE 3

This is the way we wash our clothes, wash our clothes, wash our clothes, This is the way we wash our clothes so ear - ly Mon - day morn - ing.

EXAMPLE 4

Lit - tle Sal - ly Sau - cer, sit - ting in the wa - ter, Rise, Sal-ly, rise, Sal-ly; Wipe a-way your tears, Sal-ly, Turn to the east, Sal-ly; Turn to the west, Sal-ly; Turn to the one that you love the best, Sal-ly!

EXAMPLE 5

A tis - ket, a tas - ket, a green and yel - low bas - ket, I wrote a let - ter to my love and on the way I lost it! I lost it, I lost it, yes, on the way I lost it! A lit - tle dog - gie picked it up and put it in his pock - et!

EXAMPLE 6

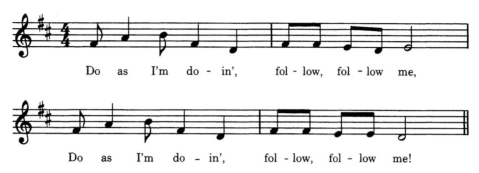

Do   as   I'm   do - in',   fol - low,   fol - low   me,

Do   as   I'm   do - in',   fol - low,   fol - low   me!

EXAMPLE 7

My   fair   la - dy! ———

EXAMPLE 8

I'm   the   king   of   the   cas - tle   and   you're   the   dir - ty   ras - cal!

Folk Dances

For children in grades three to six, there are many folk dances that are part of North America's heritage. "Old Joe Clark," "Yankee Doodle," "Pop Goes the Weasel," and "Old Brass Wagon" were all danced in earlier days to celebrate barn raisings, weddings, holidays, or just Saturday nights. Today, they can provide children with relaxation and pleasure as a part of the music curriculum.

Folk dances for older children are basically of three types: circles, including double and triple circles ("I've Been to Haarlem"); squares ("Old Brass Wagon"); and facing lines, or contradances ("The Noble Duke of York"). Many of the same steps and formations—the "right arm swing" and the do-si-do, for example—occur in all three kinds of dances.

Most basic steps are best taught in the circle formation and then transferred to squares or lines. One large circle is easier to contain and control than four squares or two lines.

The author believes that children should learn the dances of their own homeland before being led to schottisches, jigs, horas, and tarantellas. That is not to say that the latter are not very nice dances but merely to suggest that dances most closely related to the children's language, culture, and traditions are easiest to perform first. Further, the circle, square, and line dances indigenous to North America may all be performed to children's unaccompanied singing. Indeed, much of this material was originally performed that way. Dances from the European tradition, to the contrary, are generally performed to instrumental accompaniment. For these, records or tapes will be required.

Teaching Singing Games and Dances

Whenever thirty children are all out of their seats at the same time, there is the potential for mass confusion. The novice teacher may tend to become frustrated with the children's "lack of attention" and, with voice ever rising to be heard, may finally make them sit down without completing the game or dance in which they were engaged.

A little planning can forestall this:

1.   Teach the music and text for the dance or game first. Do not attempt to perform any game or dance for which the music and words are not known well.

2.   Discuss the game formation with the children while they are still seated: "Is it a circle, facing lines, square?" Discuss the space to be used: back of the room? Front? Side? Will desks have to be moved? Which desks, and where?

3.   Demonstrate any new dance motions or steps with one or two children before getting the whole class up.

4.   In games requiring partnering of boys and girls, arrange this matter-of-factly, ensuring that no child is rejected. One way to accomplish this is to have the boys stand first and form a circle. The girls then form a circle around the boys. When the boys turn to face the girls, each boy is facing his "partner." This is made more acceptable by the fact that in most games, partners change on every verse. During a game, each child will probably dance with five or six other children. Once children realize this, any objection to initially assigned partners tends to stop.

5.   Use the game song to get the children from their desks into the game formation and from the game formation back to their seats.

"Put the song in your voices and the beat in your feet. By the time you finish the first verse, be in your game formation." [Singing] "One, two, ready, go!"

6.   If, in spite of all these precautions, disorder makes it necessary to stop a game have children return to their seats and discuss with them what happened.

"Why did we have to stop?" "What can we do next time to keep that from happening?"

Games should be relaxed and happy occasions. Order need not be rigid, but the teacher must have a sense of having the children with him or her, of being the one "in charge." Dance is a disciplined activity. One child acting silly in a square-dance formation can ruin the dance for the seven others. He or she should not be allowed to do so. Often, peer pressure is all that is needed to correct such situations.

ACTIVITIES

1. Choose a singing game suitable for five-, six-, or seven-year-olds from a series book or another source listed in this chapter. Write a detailed plan for teaching it.

2. Choose a folk dance suitable for grade three, four, five, or six from a series book or another source listed in this chapter. Write a detailed plan for teaching it.

3. Teach the game or dance you choose to your class.

CREATIVE MOVEMENT

Nothing was ever created from nothing. Any creative movement draws on past movement experiences and observations. The more experiences and observations a child has had, the more "creative" his or her movements will seem. If the child's perceptions are based on rock videos, we can expect that to be reflected; if ballet lessons are a weekly occurrence in the child's life, we can expect to see that influence creative endeavors. All children who have had opportunity to play singing games and dances bring that movement vocabulary to creative experiences.

It is in the transferring and transforming of past experiences to new musical settings that "creation" occurs. The richer the background of the child, the more inventive he or she is likely to be. It is the job of the school to see that a core of experiences exists from which children can create. If games and dances of the type suggested earlier in this chapter are taught regularly, children will have such a core.

Creative Movement with Five- , Six- , and Seven-Year-Olds

Creative movement may be done to singing, to piano accompaniment, or to taped or recorded music. Whatever musical material is chosen, the teacher must have listened to it carefully and made some preliminary decisions as to what its most obvious characteristics are. Those decisions should be flexible, since children may well perceive the music differently, but some thought in advance of the lesson is still advisable.

After playing the music for the children while they quietly listen, discuss with them the character of the music and the movement possibilities suggested by the music:

"How did the music make you want to move?"

Sway	Stamp
Skip	March
Gallop	Slide
Whirl	Leap
Hop	Jump
Tiptoe	

Draw as many ideas as possible from them. Discuss the ones that fit well and the ones that do not seem particularly appropriate: stamping, for example, to very soft music. The idea that movement should reflect the music is one some children do not immediately perceive.

When a number of possibilities have been discussed and, perhaps, placed on the chalkboard, play the music once more and allow the children to move to it, using one or more of the suggested ideas, or any other they may wish to try.

At the end of the first experience with this particular piece of music, bring them back together to discuss and evaluate which movements they felt fit well and which less well.

On another day, soon after, review these activities and add the dimensions of body positions in space, possible movement direction, and use of other body parts:

"Yesterday everyone stood erect to move. Are there any other positions we could use?"

Bend over	Stretch tall
Crawl	Slither
	Etc.

"Yesterday, everyone moved only forward. How else could we move?"

Backwards	Sideways

"What parts of your body could move to the music, besides your feet and legs?"

Heads	Arms
Hands	Torso
Hips	*Etc.*

"How can we move our bodies standing in one place?"

Push	Pull
Swing	Bounce
Bend	Stretch
Twist	Shake

At this point, the teacher should play the music again so that children have opportunity to incorporate some of these "new" ideas. Again, the results should be discussed at the end of the experience.

As children have increased experience with creative movement, less teacher direction will be necessary. However, the children should hear the music to which movement is to be done before they move to it, so that they can make informed movement decisions, and there should always be evaluative discussion after the movement experience.

The same piece of music should be used several times with children. Increased familiarity with the music results in more creative movement.

Music for movement does not have to be chosen from commercial "music for movement" sources. Any music may be used for it: Bach fugues, Brahms waltzes, Gregorian chants, synthesizer compositions, and others. The more varied the musical material, the more inventive the children are likely to become.[2]

ACTIVITIES

Choose a composition to use for a creative movement lesson. Listen to it. Write down your ideas about what movements suit it, and plan the questions you will ask the children to guide their creative movement to it. Plan your evaluative questions for the end of the experience also.

MOVEMENT FOR SPECIFIC TEACHING PURPOSES

Any musical element can be illustrated through movement. Movement may be used to lead children to musical learning about the fundamental characteristics of beat, rhythm, and meter; melody; form; simultaneous sounds (harmony); and dynamics, tempo, and timbre.

Beat, Rhythm, and Meter

Clapping, tapping, stepping, skipping, and conducting are all movements that may be used to help children learn more about duration. Through these movements, children discover "how songs move" and infer concepts about rhythm, beat, and meter.

The earliest specific motions to music should be done to illustrate words of songs or rhymes: rowing the boat, rocking the baby, pushing the clouds away, showing the mouse running up the clock. The teacher may demonstrate these motions rhythmically while saying the rhyme or singing the song. Children will at first imitate the teacher's actions but later will be able to perform them independently and even to create new actions for them. This kind of "play" should both precede and continue during later, more specific performances of beat and rhythm.

---

[2]For many further creative suggestions, see Lois Choksy, Robert M. Abramson, Avon E. Gillespie, and David Woods, *Teaching Music in the Twentieth Century* (Englewood Cliffs, N. J.: Prentice-Hall, 1986), and Lois Choksy and David Brummitt, *120 Singing Games and Dances* (Englewood Cliffs, N. J.: Prentice-Hall, 1987).

When children are using such motions accurately on the beat, the teacher may begin to have them "tap the beat," using a large, free-arm motion with hands slapping lightly on thighs. This motion may be performed while either sitting or standing. Five-year-olds can tap the beat while singing. Tapping the beat should be a part of every music lesson in kindergarten and first grade. As children mature, this large motion may be made smaller and more contained. By third grade, it should consist of fingertips lightly tapping on desks while singing, and by sixth grade, it should no longer be necessary for the beat to be seen or heard. It should by that time have been internalized to the point where a steady beat can be maintained by the children during singing and playing without the visual or aural demonstration of beat.

Young children's stepping is less secure and controlled than their tapping. They should be asked to "step the beat" to songs only after they are correctly tapping it, and in the first few beat-stepping experiences, they should step and tap in unison. The tapping helps them know when to stop.

When beat tapping and stepping are being performed with ease, children may be led to focus on accented beats, the beats that determine meter. Some variation of the thigh-tapping motion will be needed for this—perhaps, slapping laps for the accented beats and tapping lightly for unaccented beats (Example 9). Through this activity, children can discover "how the music is moving":

"Are the beats moving in groups of twos, threes, or fours?"

They are determining *Meter*

EXAMPLE 9

At later grades, meter should be illustrated through conducting (see Ch. 9, pp. 100–102, for conducting gestures).

Rhythm   Rhythm can be illustrated by clapping "the way the words go." Later, children will be able to step the beat and clap the rhythm to familiar songs while singing.

Meter   The preceding activities should be performed first with simple duple and quadruple meters ($\frac{2}{4}$, $\frac{4}{4}$) and only later with triple meter ($\frac{3}{4}$). Triple is a less common meter in English-language children's music and is less obviously related to linguistic stresses.

Compound meter ($\frac{6}{8}$), on the other hand, is extremely closely related to language. Most English-language nursery rhymes are in $\frac{6}{8}$. This meter has a very different feel from $\frac{2}{4}$, $\frac{3}{4}$, or $\frac{4}{4}$ and should from the beginning involve a different kind of movement. Skipping, galloping, and swaying are good movements for songs and rhymes in $\frac{6}{8}$.

By always stepping for music in simple meter ($\frac{2}{4}$, $\frac{4}{4}$) and skipping for music in compound meter ($\frac{6}{8}$), the teacher is preparing the children so that later they will be able to aurally distinguish between these two types of meters. (See Ch. 9, pp. 103–6, for further discussion of simple and compound meters.)

Melody

At the simplest level, children may show by arm motions or body positions when sounds are higher, when lower, and when the same in easy two-note and three-note songs (Example 10). Later, they may incorporate motions to show "highest sounds" and "lowest sounds" in wider-range melodies (Example 11).

EXAMPLE 10

Bounce high, bounce low, bounce the ball to Shi - lo.

EXAMPLE 11

The first one, the sec - ond one, the third fol - low me!

At somewhat more advanced levels, children may show specific melodic contours with hands and arms and may illustrate the broad lines of that contour through body position in creative movement.

For specific learning about melody to be learned or reinforced in this way through movement, the children should have opportunity both to discuss the melodic characteristics of the music before moving and, afterwards, to evaluate how effectively their movements illustrated these characteristics.

Form

One of the easiest aspects of music to reflect in movement is form. Initially, a simple arm-arcing motion may be used to illustrate phrase length (Example 12). Later, children skipping in a circle can change direction on each phrase of the song.

EXAMPLE 12

Here we go loo - by loo,___ Here we go loo - by light,___

Here we go loo - by loo,___ All on a Sa - tur - day night!

At the next level, children may be expected to identify which phrases are the same and which different and to illustrate that sameness or difference in their movement, whether they are simply stepping or skipping in a circle or performing more complex free movements.

A song in *abac* form, such as "Looby Loo," for example, may be performed as follows:

a	Skip clockwise	"Here we go looby loo"
b	Skip counterclockwise	"Here we go looby light"
a	Skip clockwise	"Here we go looby loo"
c	Skip toward center of circle	"All on a Saturday night"

When children can identify and respond physically to "same" and "different" in music, the idea of "similar" should be introduced (Example 13). When a phrase is similar, *something* about it is the same, and that sameness should be reflected in the movement, while something else about it is different, and that difference, too, must be reflected in the movement. In Example 13, the children might continue to step or march—this would illustrate the sameness of the rhythm and meter—but might use a lower body position to illustrate the "differentness" of the melody. The second phrase in this piece is a sequence of the first, stated in a lower place. The children's movement should reflect this.

EXAMPLE 13

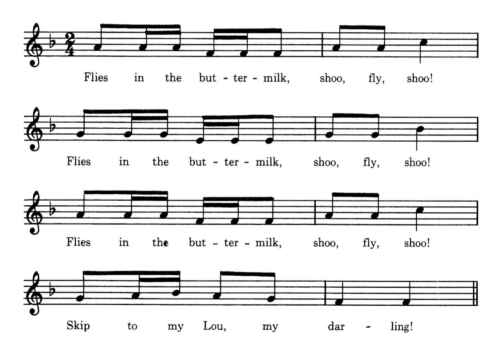

Flies in the but-ter-milk, shoo, fly, shoo!

Flies in the but-ter-milk, shoo, fly, shoo!

Flies in the but-ter-milk, shoo, fly, shoo!

Skip to my Lou, my dar - ling!

Large forms—movements of symphonies, theme and variations, rondos—can all be illustrated clearly and imaginatively through movement once children can identify and physically illustrate "same," "different," and "similar" in songs.

Simultaneous Sounds (Harmony)

Two or more pitches sounding together create what is usually referred to as harmony. Perhaps, the simplest setting in which two or more pitches sound at the same time is the round or the canon (Example 14). The form of rounds and canons can be illustrated easily and with delightful effect through movement.

EXAMPLE 14

Are you sleep - ing,   Are   you   sleep - ing,

Broth - er   John,   Broth - er   John?

Morn-ing bells are ring - ing,   Morn-ing bells are ring - ing,

Ding,   dang,   dong.   Ding,   dang,   dong.

First, the class should decide upon a series of simple movements, one movement for each different phrase. For example:

a	Step clockwise	"Are you sleeping, are you sleeping?"
b	Step counterclockwise	"Brother John, Brother John"
c	4 steps forward	"Morning . . . "
d	4 steps back	"Ding . . . "

These can be further elaborated by adding arm and body motions to show "sleeping" (heads against hands to show sleeping); "Brother John" (hands in front in a praying motion); "Morning bells... (pulling the bell ropes); "Ding..."(swaying to show the bell movement).

To this point, the movement has simply illustrated the form of the song—*abac*. However, when the motions are being performed well in unison, the song should be sung as a round, with two circles, one performing the actions *after* the other. Later, three or more groups may be used, each performing to its own singing of the melody. This may be done with four separate circles or with concentric circles of increasing size—four children in the innermost circle, eight in the circle around them, twelve in the next one, and so on. This clear physical and visual demonstration of how canons work is worth a thousand words about canons.

A class that can move in canon will have little difficulty moving to themes and countermelodies in a Bach fugue. Counterpoint can be made visible through movement.

Chordal harmony also can be demonstrated with movement. Children readily perceive the incompleteness of certain kinds of cadences—I V^7; I IV V; I V vi—and can show this feeling of incompleteness through movement which is sharply contrasted to the movement demanded by a final cadence: V^7 I; IV V^7 I. They do not have to know harmony or chord designations to respond accurately physically to different kinds of cadences.

Tempo, Dynamics, and Timbre—The "Expressive" Elements

Movement may also be used to present and reinforce concepts about tempo, dynamics, and timbre.

Tempo Tempo is not fastness or slowness but, rather, the relative fastness or slowness of the beat in music. To reflect tempo accurately, children must be able first to distinguish the beat from surface rhythm and then to move accurately to the beat.

Changing from a slow large step for a pattern ♩ ♩ ♩ ♩ to a running step for ♫ ♫ ♫ ♫ is not a response to tempo but to surface rhythm. To help children perceive this difference, one simple technique is to have them sing and play a game at the tempo they normally would; then, carefully set a much slower beat and ask them to do it again, in that tempo. Later, do it in a faster tempo. Discuss the changes in movement necessitated by the changes in tempo.

If they can change the tempo of familiar singing games and respond with accurate movement to those changes, they are more likely to be able to distinguish surface rhythmic changes from actual tempo changes in recorded music to which they are asked to move.

Dynamics Movement responses to dynamics may be as simple as tiptoeing when the music is softer and stamping when it is louder. However, at more advanced levels, motions to illustrate dynamics and dynamic changes can be extremely subtle. A syncopated rhythm with dynamic accent could be shown by a simple motion of the shoulders; a crescendo could be illustrated by moving from a closed to an open position physically. Expansive large motions are generally associated with louder music, more restrained inward-turned motions with softer music. Often, children will illustrate these principles without having discussed them. The teacher should be quick to use such intuitive movement as a basis for generalization.

Timbre One of the most difficult aspects of music to talk about is tone color—the difference in the sound of two instruments or voices producing the same pitch. In spite of this, timbre is one of the musical characteristics most easily perceived by children.[3]

No one could fail to hear that the sound of an oboe is quite different from that of a violin or a trumpet. Reflecting this difference in movement is perhaps not as obvious as reflecting dynamic or tempo changes, but children's attention should be focused on the different timbral effects in music to which they are moving.

CONCLUSION

Movement can add immeasurably to children's enjoyment and understanding of music. It can become the impetus for learning in any element of music. Skills and concepts in melody, duration, form, harmony, tempo, dynamics, and timbre can be introduced or reinforced through movement.

Songs, examples played on piano and other classroom instruments, and recordings can provide the musical stimulus for movement activities, although it should be noted that younger children tend to move more accurately to their own self-produced music (singing) than to external sound sources (piano, recordings).

Singing games and dances or other movement activities can provide a release from tension within the school day that allows children to return refreshed to other activities, whether those activities are musical or nonmusical.

[3]In recent study by Louisa Izzo at The University of Calgary, intended to focus on children's ability to distinguish between higher and lower pitches, the children responded not to differences in pitch but to difference in timbre. The study had to be redesigned.

ACTIVITIES

Choose a song or a piece of recorded music with which to illustrate a basic principle in one element of music. Plan a movement experience for children, using this piece of music.

To focus attention on the specific element, what guide questions will you ask before the children move to the piece? How will you and the class evaluate the experience?

CHAPTER 5

ACTIVITIES THROUGH WHICH CHILDREN LEARN MUSIC
Playing Instruments

Instrumental experience can add dimension and variety to the school music program. While basic skills and concepts are perhaps better taught through singing, playing instruments can offer valuable reinforcement of those skills and concepts.

Children are fascinated by instruments from an early age. Most two-year-olds would rather bang on kitchen pots and pans than play with commercial toys, and what four-year-old can be long in the room with a piano without pressing the keys? This natural interest and curiosity about instrumental sounds can be channeled, fostered, and further developed in the school music class.

CLASSROOM INSTRUMENTS

Instruments for classroom use fall generally into four categories:

- Unpitched or rhythm instruments
- Pitched or melody instruments
- Chording or harmony instruments
- Keyboard instruments

Some instruments exist in more than one of these categories. Each category will be discussed in turn in the following pages.

UNPITCHED OR RHYTHM INSTRUMENTS

There was a time (the author hopes it is past) when "rhythm bands" were common in the schools. Each child in a class was assigned an instrument—often the only rhythm instrument that child ever got to play—and the "band" played along with a recording of dubious music, conducted with questionable skill by the teacher or a classmate. The whole was rehearsed for weeks and finally presented to parents in the "Spring Program." Children had little or nothing to say about which instruments should play, or when or how, and little, if any, musical learning resulted from the activity.

Today, rhythm instruments are more commonly used as enrichment for the general music class. They are introduced one at a time and are used initially as accompaniment.

ACCOMPANIMENT FOR SONG

The children may use finger cymbals, triangles, or gong to chime the hours.

ACCOMPANIMENT FOR RHYME

Engine, Engine Number Nine,
Going down Chicago Line,
If the train goes off the track,
Do I get my money back?

Here, sandblocks could be used throughout to represent the chugging sound of the train, and later, a cowbell could be the signal for "All aboard!"

ACCOMPANIMENT FOR MOVEMENT

Hand drum or tone block can be used to play the children's walking beat.

As each type of instrument is introduced, care should be taken that all children have opportunity to experiment with it and to learn to hold and play it correctly. The various ways of producing sounds on instruments should be explored and discussed. This will probably take several lessons for each instrument.

When three or more kinds of instruments have been introduced, small "ensembles" may be formed, and songs and rhymes may be "orchestrated" by the children. These orchestrations may be placed on charts by the teacher (see Example 1), although they should not be formalized in this way until children have had ample opportunity to experiment and find the ways they like best.

EXAMPLE 1   Children's Orchestration Chart

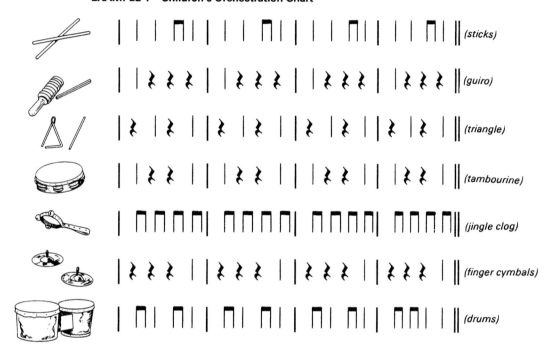

Rhythm instruments may be purchased by individual item or in complete sets, or they may be constructed by teacher and children. Commercial sets generally come with sturdy storage boxes and offer a good variety of basic instruments.

The usual rhythm instrument set includes sticks, woodblocks, triangles, tambourines, jingle bells, rattles, sandblocks, drums, and cymbals. Some may also include claves, maracas, and a gong. These may be supplemented by special orders for numerous more exotic instruments, ranging from small slit drums to full timpani.

While the playing technique for most rhythm instruments is fairly obvious, a few words about some special characteristics or problems may prove helpful.

Sticks   Generally, one stick is simply tapped against the other. However, some sticks are ridged. A plain stick may be rubbed along a ridged one to produce another kind of sound.

Triangles   Triangles are held suspended by a ribbon or a knob. They tend to twist and turn. To prevent this, children may hold them by the metal rather than by the knob. The resulting sound is dull and lifeless. When the triangle is introduced, the teacher should stress the need for it to hang freely so that it can vibrate, and children should compare the sound produced with and without the triangle hanging freely.

Rhythm Instrument Set

Tambourines   The holding hand should be on the rim rather than against the head. Different sounds may be produced by tapping with fingertips, with heel of hand, at the rim, or in the center. Other sounds can be obtained by rubbing the thumb across the head or jangling the instrument.

Finger Cymbals   Children love the clear, bell-like sound of these instruments but finger cymbals are not the easiest of rhythm instruments to play, because they are very small. Like the triangle, they must be held by a cord or a knob rather than by the metal part to vibrate freely. One cymbal is held stationary and is struck in a descending motion with the other. They are not "crashed together" like big orchestral cymbals but are held in hanging position.

For instruments requiring two hands, one to hold and one to strike (triangle, tambourine, finger cymbals), the striking hand should be the child's dominant one, the one with which he or she writes.

Drums   The best way for young children first to play drums is with hands, not with sticks. Drums, if struck in the middle as children tend to do, produce a flat, dull tone. They should, instead, be struck near the edge. When the instrument is first introduced, these two playing modes and their sounds should be demonstrated and discussed.

Constructing Rhythm Instruments

For the school that does not have and cannot purchase commercial rhythm instruments, quite satisfactory ones can be constructed by teacher and children. Thick dowels may be cut into lengths for rhythm sticks, and sandpaper may be cemented to wooden blocks for sand blocks. Children can supply plastic lidded boxes or cans with dried beans in them for rattles. Seed pods found in some locales also work well as rattles. If the teacher encourages the children to "find" natural instruments in their environment and use discardable household items (boxes, bags, tins) to create new instruments, the results can be quite interesting. The teacher can give further direction by asking the children to collect examples of "wood sounds" or "metal sounds," or to find "something we can play by striking" or "something we can play by shaking." Even for the class that has a full set of rhythm instruments, such activities can provide a meaningful learning experience.

Most rhythm instruments will be introduced to children in kindergarten and first grade. However, rhythm instruments may be used effectively throughout the elementary school years to add interest to songs and to accompany movement.

PITCHED OR MELODY INSTRUMENTS

There are numerous classroom instruments on which children may play melodies, among them the following:

BARRED INSTRUMENTS

Tone or resonator bells
Glockenspiels
Xylophones
Metallophones

WIND INSTRUMENTS

Bottles
Song flutes
Recorders

Barred Instruments

Resonator Bells

Perhaps the easiest melody instruments for young children are resonator bells. At first glance, these look rather like a boxed xylophone; however, each bar is essentially a separate instrument—a rectangular plastic resonating box on which a metal bar rests suspended by rubber fasteners. The bar is played with a rubber mallet. The pitch is usually accurate and the tone soft, mellow, and bell-like—ideal for accompanying young voices.

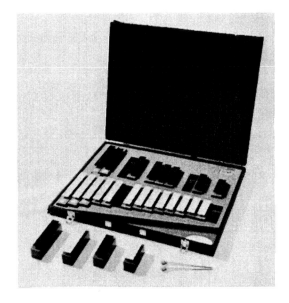

Resonator Bells

The teacher may take from the box only the bars needed to play a particular song, for example A, C, and D for "Rain, Rain, Go Away." Each bar is marked with the name of its note. In some of the newer sets of resonator bells, both the note's name and its position on the staff are shown right on each bar.

Fixed Chromatic Bell Sets

Fixed chromatic bells, like resonator bells, are made of metal bars, but they are fastened to wooden or plastic strips in a scale order from lowest (on the left) to highest (on the right). "Black notes" are situated above "white notes" much as they are on a piano keyboard. The individual bars are not generally meant to be removable, although children sometimes find a way.

The full chromatic arrangement tends to be unduly complicated for early instrumental experience.

Orff Instruments

German composer Carl Orff (1895–1982) developed for use with children a series of instruments that have a unique tone quality. They are extremely suitable for accompanying children's singing. They include glockenspiels, xylophones, and metallophones.

Chromatic Bell Set

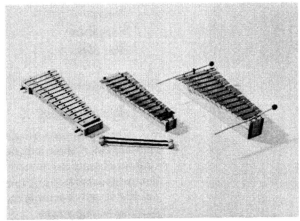

Glockenspiels

Xylophones

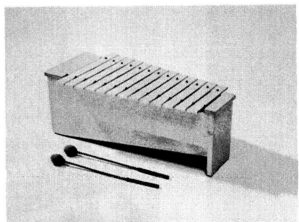

Metallophones

Bass glockenspiels, xylophones, and metallophones are generally used to play accompaniments rather than melodies.

Teachers trained in Orff techniques use all these instruments in a special way as part of the "process" of Orff pedagogy.[1] However, they can be used in any music class to provide the children with instrumental experience. Like resonator bells, barred Orff instruments may be prepared by the teacher so that only the notes needed to play a particular song are on the instrument when the child approaches it to play.

Orff instruments are meant to be played with soft felt mallets held loosely in both hands, using a free, bouncing sort of touch. Unless one is specifically following an Orff approach, the general process for playing a song on any barred instrument might be as follows:

- Sing the song with words.
- Sing the song using absolute note names (musical ABC's).
- Play the song while singing the note names. (Use two mallets and both hands.)

Children should be given time to "find the melody" even on prepared instruments. If a class has used solfa and rhythm duration syllables previously, singing with these is a useful intermediary step between singing with words and singing with absolute note names, and before playing.

Wind Instruments

Bottles

The simplest wind instruments are homemade ones—made from bottles of various sizes. The teacher should ask children to bring in glass bottles of as many sizes as possible. When these are filled with varying amounts of water, full two-octave chromatic scales may be constructed, although for earliest teaching purposes, a pentatonic scale is sufficient. By blowing across the tops of the bottles, the children can produce pitches, which can be refined with considerable accuracy simply by pouring out or adding water.

Choose a song the children know extremely well, and assign a scale pitch to each child in the group. (This can be done in solfa or with ABC's.) Each time that child's note occurs in the song, he or she must produce it by blowing across the top of his or her bottle. Several groups may work in this way on different songs. The results are unlikely to win any awards for beauty, but everyone has a great deal of fun, and in the process, some important concepts and skills may be developed and refined:

- The concept that larger instruments (bottles) produce lower sounds and smaller instruments (bottles) produce higher sounds
- The understanding that when we add water, we are reducing the space in which the air can vibrate, so the pitch will be higher
- The understanding that when we pour out water, we are increasing the space in which the air can vibrate, so the pitch will be lower
- The skill of following a piece of music closely enough to come in every time and on time with the *so* or G

"Bottle choirs" are best used with older children, grade four and above.

[1]See Lois Choksy, Robert M. Abramson, Avon Gillespie, and David Woods, *Teaching Music in the Twentieth Century* (Englewood Cliffs, N.J.: Prentice-Hall, 1986), for a full discussion of the Orff approach.

Song Flutes and Recorders

For many years, small plastic wind instruments variously know as Songflutes, Tonettes, and Flutophones were widely found in the schools. They were used primarily for preband instrumental training—as a way of helping children fasten printed notation to at least a fingering or a place on an instrument, if not to sound. They were reasonably effective, used for that purpose. However, their tone quality was often painful to hear.

Recorders, on the other hand, can have a very pleasant tone. Recorders were not found in many schools previously because, being made of wood, they were very expensive. Today, reasonably good quality recorders made of plastic may be purchased quite reasonably in class sets, and the mouthpieces can be sterilized, so that a class set may be retained by the school and used for a number of years. It should be noted that many times, parents are more than willing to pay the small cost of a recorder for their children. Where possible, this is preferable, because the child gets to keep the instrument with which he or she has worked.

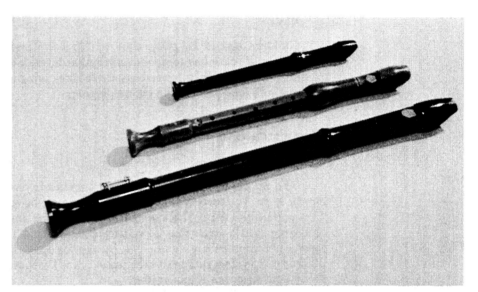

Soprano, Alto, and Tenor Recorders

It is the author's belief that every child should have at least four months of recorder study during the elementary school years, and that, ideally, this should happen around fourth or fifth grade. At this age, the small motor facility needed for correct fingering is present, the missing teeth of first and second grade have been replaced, and, it is to be hoped, some minimal level of music reading is occurring in the singing classes.

After an initial four-month period of class recorder instruction, some children will doubtless show more interest than others in continuing. Those who wish to could then become a special "recorder club"—an extracurricular activity.

There are numerous good recorder books available,[2] but children enjoy playing songs they know. Here is one process for using children's familiar songs for initial recorder playing:

[2]For example, Carol King, *Recorder Routes: A Guide to Introducing Soprano Recorder* (Memphis, Tenn.: Memphis Musicraft, 1978).

1. The teacher chooses several three-note songs the children know.
2. With each song in turn the children
   a. Sing with words.
   b. Sing in solfa or with ABC's.
   Steps a and b are done with the recorder in "rest position."
3. The children then place the recorder mouthpiece just below the mouth, resting it on the chin, and sing the fingering—"3-2-1," and so on.
4. Finally, the children place the mouthpiece at the lips and play.

This approach has the advantage that the children, knowing the tunes they are playing, are immediately aware of musical mistakes and are motivated to correct them.

The two most frequent corrections needed are "Blow more lightly" and "Make sure your fingers are covering the holes."

This approach may be used in combination with recorder books as well, by simply having students singing each exercise or piece before they play it.

CHORDING OR HARMONY INSTRUMENTS

Any instrument may be used to accompany singing, but certain instruments, by their vary nature, seem principally to be intended for accompanying. Among these are the alto and bass xylophones and metallophones and stringed instruments such as Autoharp, dulcimer, ukulele, and guitar.

Accompanying Singing with Barred Instruments

Orff instruments, the bass xylophones and metallophones, are customarily used to play a simple Bordun to accompany pentatonic melodies (Example 2). This may also be played with left and right hand alternating (Example 3).

EXAMPLE 2

EXAMPLE 3

Although this basic Orff accompaniment is an attractive addition to many pentatonic tunes, take care not to use it with any song that implies more complex harmonies (a subdominant, for example).

The "alto" Orff instruments may be added to the Bordun, playing some rhythmic variation on a minor third or on octaves for further interest (Example 4). Over this, voices and soprano instruments carry the melody (Example 5).

EXAMPLE 4

EXAMPLE 5 "Rain, Come Wet Me" (score for soprano, alto, and bass Orff instruments)

Rain, come wet me, Sun, come dry me, Keep a-way, pret-ty girls, Don't come nigh me!

Autoharps

Autoharps are, as the name implies, harp-shaped instruments that are somewhat automatic in the way in which they produce chords. Essentially, they are a resonating box, small enough for an adult or an older child to hold on the lap, with strings stretched across the entire surface and a number of bars with chord designations written on them—C, G, F, D, and so on. The performer presses the bars with one hand and strums the strings with the other.

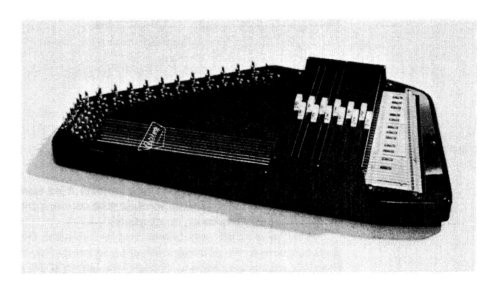

Autoharp

Following the chord markings given in many music series texts or in any guitar book, theoretically even the least musically astute teacher or student should be able to use the Autoharp to accompany singing. The reality is far from this. Autoharps, while easy to play, are difficult and time consuming to tune, and they tend to need tuning every time they are played. No one should try to sing with an untuned Autoharp. Recently, an electronic version of the Autoharp has been developed. It appears to hold its tuning better.

The Dulcimer

This simple four-stringed instrument has long been traditional for accompanying folk music. Melodies may be played on it by sliding a small wooden bar along its strings with one hand and plucking them with the other. Simple accompaniments of open fifths similar to the Orff Bordun may also be played on dulcimers to accompany singing.

Dulcimer

Dulcimers have the advantage that they are both easy to play and easy to tune. Further, there are relatively inexpensive kits available for building these instruments in the classroom—some of wood and others of heavy cardboard. Even the cardboard ones produce a reasonably acceptable sound.

Ukuleles

These banjolike chording instruments have been very popular in some areas. Clubs have been formed and ukulele "bands" of thirty or more young players have performed their I, IV, and V chord accompaniments while singing "Shine On, Harvest Moon," "Carolina in the Morning," and other equally dated and forgettable melodies. At best, these instruments have an unpleasant twang, and at worst, they are keeping children from experiencing worthwhile music. Their principal value appears to be that they are less expensive than guitars.

Guitar

Anyone who can be taught to play a ukulele can be taught to play a guitar, and the tone quality of even a cheap guitar is vastly superior. The guitar is a good chording instrument in the hands of either teacher or older child. With three simple chords (I, IV, V) and a capo, the performer can accompany literally hundreds of folksongs in numerous keys.

The guitar is perhaps the most popular of folk instruments. In most schools, there will be at least one teacher with a rudimentary knowledge of guitar. This person can be used as a resource for other teachers or children wishing to learn.

KEYBOARD INSTRUMENTS

The piano is, of course, the keyboard instrument available in nearly every school. It should be used very sparingly to accompany singing in the early grades when children are still learning to sing accurately. However, in the upper grades, an artistic accompaniment, well played by either student or teacher, can add to the beauty of a performance. Piano lessons are not usually offered as a part of the school music program, although there have been some very successful instances of piano classes (group instruction) in public schools. However, even without the existence of piano classes, the piano may be used, as may any instrument, to reinforce musical learning and to enrich musical experiences. Children who have learned to sing a I–V progression as accompaniment to a song can learn to play the same progression on the keyboard. Melodies that can be played on xylophones can be easily transferred to piano.

The near future holds promise of much wider use of keyboards in class music instruction. As electronic keyboards become less expensive and more accessible, it is not unreasonable to predict that they will find their way into classroom music.

ORCHESTRAL AND BAND INSTRUMENTS

Across the United States and Canada, practices vary widely with respect to elementary orchestra and band programs. In many schools, there is no elementary instrumental program of any kind; in others, instruction in band or orchestral instruments may begin as early as fourth grade. Needless to say, these latter programs demand qualified music teachers.

Such programs are almost always selective rather than general. Children must usually rent their instruments and, often, have to "audition" to receive group "band" instruction. Band instrument and string instrument programs seldom seem to coexist in the same school. Perhaps, this is more a result of individual teachers' training and abilities than of school or community wishes. However, it is worth noting that instrumental programs in the schools of the United States historically had their birth at the secondary school in the need to send the football team to glory. (Who ever heard of a marching string orchestra?) Still today, band programs and secondary instrumental programs far outnumber elementary ones. Both band and string programs tend to be aimed at the "select few" at whatever age they begin.

One exception to this was a program widespread in the schools of Baltimore County, Maryland, for many years—one that could well serve as a model for all elementary music instrumental experience.

The Exploratory Music Program

The Exploratory Music Program, developed by music supervisor Nicholas Geriak and instrumental helping teacher Michael Prevas, brought first-hand instrumental experience to every fourth-grade child in more than 100 schools during a period of some twenty years. A number of class sets of clarinets, trumpets, and violins were purchased by the district. Large portable storage boxes were made to house them. Each class set was sent to a school for a period of approximately two months. During that time, instruction on that instrument was given to all fourth-grade students in that school, twice weekly. Lessons were carefully structured to be uniform throughout the district. The emphasis was on "exploring" the instrument and on improvising with it rather than on learning notes and performing exercises.

At the end of two months, the sets were exchanged with another school and the children were given two months of exploration and discovery with an instrument from another instrumental family. By the end of the year, all fourth-grade children had had opportunity to hold, examine, and produce sounds, and at a simple level, play a stringed, a woodwind, and a brass instrument.

One result of this program was that bands and orchestras in the district had unprecedented enrollment. Another, perhaps more important result was that in the course of exploring the instruments, children learned enough to make more informed decisions about which instruments they wanted to play. No longer did everyone choose trumpet because it was shiny.

Most important, however, all children had first-hand experiences with orchestral instruments. Such experience probably does more to positively influence attitudes and appreciation of instrumental music than all the recordings one could ever play to children.

CONCLUSION

Instrumental experience can greatly enrich the school music program if instruments are introduced individually over a period of time and if children are guided to explore and experiment with instrumental sounds rather than simply being taught "how to play" instruments. Performance should not be the focus of elementary school instrumental study, although it may be a by-product. The purpose of such study should be discovery of principles and the refining of skills. At the elementary school level, it is process rather than product that should be at the heart of any instrumental experience.

ACTIVITIES

1. Put together a set of rhythm instruments entirely from handmade and found sources. Orchestrate a piece of folk music for these instruments.

2. Choose three songs from a school music series text. Using resonator bells, create a simple second part for each.

3. Using soprano, alto, and bass Orff instruments, improvise or compose a simple accompaniment for "Rain, Rain, Go Away." Work small groups to do this.

CHAPTER 6

ACTIVITIES THROUGH WHICH CHILDREN LEARN MUSIC
Musical Reading and Writing

Although few people in the twentieth century question the necessity for linguistic literacy, a surprising number of people responsible for the education of the young still appear to harbor doubts as to the value of musical literacy and see no need for including it as a goal of music education. Perhaps, that is because for many years in North America, musical literacy has been equated with looking at a note on a printed page and pushing the corresponding button or key—an action from eye to hand with little passing through the brain other than a superficial linking of the two. This is not music reading. Music reading involves (1) seeing a musical pattern or line, (2) hearing the sounds in one's head, and then (3) producing those sounds instrumentally or vocally. Without the second, inner-hearing, step, music reading is simply a mechanical action—something that could be performed more easily, and probably more musically, by a machine than by a human being.

Genuine musical literacy involves far more than simply producing correct sounds. It implies an ability to look at notation and think sound, to hear sound and be able to jot down the corresponding notation, and to use the symbol system of music to put down one's own musical ideas. This is no more and no less than is expected in language instruction, and music is essentially a language.

It should go without saying that it is not possible for the musically illiterate to teach musical reading and writing to children. A teacher who cannot read and write music cannot teach musical reading and writing any more than a teacher who can't add can teach math or one who can't speak French can teach conversational French. Over the years, numerous spurious arguments about "learning with the children" have been put forward, and more than one curriculum has been devised that attempts to teach the teachers so that they may teach children. The aim is worthy. The approach is ineffective. The teacher who wishes to teach musical literacy skills must first acquire those skills. There are courses in basic musicianship offered by nearly every university and music school in North America. Unfortunately, they are rarely required as a part of the would-be classroom teacher's training. The author strongly urges teachers without this background to acquire it.

A great deal of value may be imparted to children by the classroom teacher who is naturally musical, who has a pleasant singing voice, and who enjoys music regularly with his or her class, even if that teacher cannot read a note. For the more musically knowledgeable teacher, however, the teaching of musical literacy skills can offer many satisfactions in the forms of a higher level of musical performance and far greater musical understanding on the part of the children.

The rest of this chapter is directed to those teachers who are musically able and would like to open the doors to genuine musicianship for their children by teaching them the symbol system through which musical sounds may be preserved and communicated to others.

MUSIC-READING SYSTEMS

There are a number of systems used in North America for teaching music reading in the schools. Among them, the most prevalent used for pitch are numbers, absolute names (or fixed-*do*), and movable-*do* solfa; rhythmic reading is usually done by counting or by chanting rhythm syllables, of which there are numerous variations.

Systems of Rhythmic Reading

Notes are given mathematical rhythmic names: quarter, eighth, half, and whole notes. However, notes are not fractions, and the use of mathematics to explain music inevitably breaks down. It may be very well and good to talk about four "quarters" (♩♩♩♩) equaling a "whole" (𝅝), but what about measures with five quarters ($\frac{5}{4}$) or three half notes ($\frac{3}{2}$) or nine eighths ($\frac{9}{8}$)? Any attempt to teach music through mathematics is doomed to failure. Notes do not have "value"; rather, they have "relative durations." Any effective system for teaching rhythm must be based on this initial premise. Further, it is not possible to chant or speak rhythm names in rhythm. *Quarter* is a two-syllable word, but it represents one sound. Because of these difficulties, teachers have looked for other ways of expressing rhythmic duration.

Many band teachers in North America have long used a "counting" system such as Example 1 for teaching rhythmic notation. The children tap the beat with their feet while "counting out" the rhythm. The system has worked, more or less, for generations of school bands; however, once taught to tap the beat with their feet, children have difficulty "unlearning" the beat tapping, with the consequence that all tunes end up sounding a bit like "Marching through Georgia." Further, although such "counting" of rhythms works well enough for easy rhythms, it breaks down as more complex rhythms and meters are encountered. Further, it is a system more suitable to band than to vocal music.

EXAMPLE 1

Rhythm syllables offer an alternative to rhythmic counting. The earliest of these were devised by nineteenth-century French music theorist Jacques Chevé and were quite involved, with the syllable changing to indicate not only the relative duration of each note but also its place in the measure (see Example 2).

EXAMPLE 2

Ta   ta - tay   ta fe ti fi

This system is still used in French conservatories and in some music schools in North America. Its complexity makes it questionable for use in the public schools.

A system of reading rhythms related to and derived from the French system is the one developed by Hungarian music educators in the 1940s and further revised for use with English-speaking children.[1] It is shown in Example 3. This system has the value of simplicity. A quarter note is spoken or sung as *ta*, the eighth note as *ti*, in any position in the measure and in any meter. Long vowel sounds are used for longer notes, shorter vowels for short notes. Of all systems, this is the one probably most widely used for rhythmic reading in North American elementary schools, and it is coming into increasing use in conservatories and music schools. Rhythm reading is easy using the system (Example 4).

EXAMPLE 3

Ta   ti too   tam   ti-ka ti-ka tri-o-la toe   toom

EXAMPLE 4

Ti ti ti ti   ti ti ti ti   ti ti ti ti too,

ti ti ti ti   ti ti ti ti   ti ti ti ti too.

ta   ta   ta   ta   ti ti ti ti too,

ta   ta   ta   ta   ti ti ti ti too.

Systems of Melodic Reading

One of the common ways of introducing music reading in the elementary school is through the use of wind instruments—Songflutes or recorders. While this is prefer-

[1]For further information, see Lois Choksy, The *Kodály Method,* 2nd ed. (Englewood Cliffs, N. J.: Prentice-Hall, 1988).

able to not introducing notation at all, it does have some drawbacks. Children whose only experience with notation is through an instrument tend to relate the notation not to sound but to finger position. Even when they are asked to chant the "note names" before playing, they relate those names to places rather than to sounds. This can be circumvented by having them sing the note names on the correct pitches before playing, but teachers rarely seem to do this. Still, some learning can and does happen through such instrumental experience, and teachers who are uncomfortable with less concrete ways of teaching notation are encouraged to use the recorder in their teaching. Finger positions should not be chanted or sung, or at least should not be the only thing chanted or sung. The second space on the staff should not be thought of by children as "3," but as "A" or as "mi" in F-*do*. The first has no potential for transfer to other musical situations; both the second and the third have.

Absolute note names, the musical ABC's, are the reading tools of most private instrumental teachers. Children learn that the musical spaces (in the G clef) spell F-A-C-E and that the lines say Every Good Boy Deserves Fudge. Children memorize staff positions by name and relate those names to places on a keyboard. The system of fixed-*do* solfège used by some music schools does precisely the same except that the names used are solfège syllables, *do-re-mi*: *Do* is C, *re* is D, and so on, permanently and in any key. This system presents even more difficulties for children than absolute note names, since at least there is a different name for each note when using ABC's—G, G-sharp, G-flat—while in fixed-*do* solfège, all three of these notes are sung with the syllable *so*.

For the average person, the reading system that has proven the most accessible is movable-*do*.[2] In this system, which has been used widely in Great Britain and North America since the 1850s, key and tonality are emphasized. *Do* is the keynote in major and *la* in minor, and music is taught as tonal patterns and intervallic relationships rather than as isolated pitches.

Perhaps the most systematic English language approach to teaching musical reading and writing using movable-*do* solfa is to be found in the various North American adaptations of the Kodály Method, shown in Examples 5 and 6.

EXAMPLE 5

[2]Admittedly, this works only with tonal music and can't be used effectively with twentieth-century atonal music. But then, how much atonal music are we likely to do with fourth graders?

EXAMPLE 6

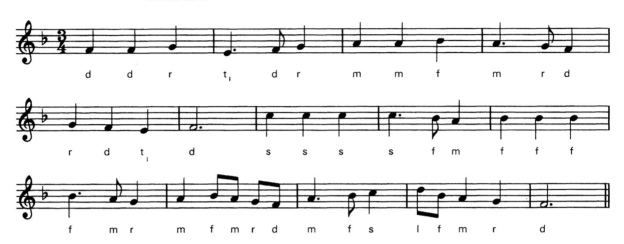

For the rest of this chapter, there will be an assumption that the teacher is using a system of rhythm duration syllables and movable-*do* solfa to guide musical reading and writing. However, the techniques suggested are usable within any music-reading system.

TEACHING LITERACY SKILLS

Any musical reading and writing should be preceded by much rote musical experience. Just as children speak long before they read, they should sing long before musical notation is introduced. The young child listens to and imitates the singing voices in his or her environment: parents, playmates, radio and television, recordings. The richer the musical surrounding, the more ready the child will be for reading and writing music.

When literacy skills are finally approached, it should be through a process involving several stages:

1.   The teacher ensures that some of the children's songs are carefully chosen to focus on specific rhythmic elements or melodic turns to be learned.

2.   The teacher focuses children's attention on a "new" pattern and asks guide questions designed to elicit all the information the children can give regarding it.

"Is the new note higher or lower than . . . ?"
"How many sounds are on the second beat?"

3.   The teacher names and shows the new rhythm or note in the context of a song phrase.

4.   The children notate what they have just learned. This "notation" consists of constructing the rhythm pattern with sticks or the melodic pattern with felt notes on individual felt staves, or it may involve notating on the staff with pencil and paper.

5.   Children read known songs containing the new material.

6.   Children read new songs containing the new material.

7.   Children use the newly learned material in improvising and composing their own rhythms or tunes.

These seven steps should be repeated for each new rhythmic figure, interval, or melodic turn taught.   They are similar to the steps involved in acquiring linguistic literacy.

Note that in this learning sequence, "writing" precedes "reading." The act of making a symbolic representation is more direct than the act of interpreting symbolic representation. Writing comes before reading because writing is a more concrete activity than reading. It is easier to recognize ♩ ♩ ♩ ♩ in print if one has written ♩ ♩ ♩ ♩.

Notice also that the first "reading" is not primavista reading but, rather, becoming familiar with the way the new learning looks in the context of previously known material. This kind of reading of songs originally taught by rote should be done frequently and with a sizable number of songs. It is at this "practice" level that the success of teaching literacy skills often breaks down, because of a lack of a sufficient number of songs and because of the teacher's mistaken notion that children "know" something because it has been "taught" in one lesson. Only after considerable practice with "reading" known songs should a song that has not previously been heard be placed before the children for reading.

Of course, the last stage of the process is "create." If the child can write and can read using the newly taught rhythmic figure or melodic turn, he or she should also be able, with guidance, to use the newly learned musical vocabulary in improvisation and composition.

Music Writing

The readiness for music writing begins the first time any kind of pictorial symbol is used to represent sound. This can happen as early as kindergarten and should happen no later than first grade.

Children can show with felt cut-outs the following things:

How many beats go by in a phrase (Example 7)

EXAMPLE 7 "Ring Around the Rosy"

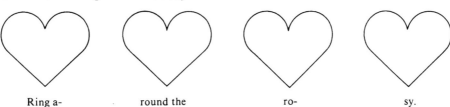

How many sounds are on each beat (Example 8)

EXAMPLE 8 "Rain, Rain, Go Away"

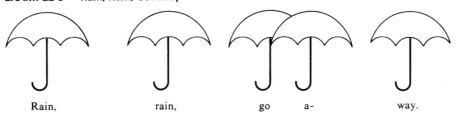

Where the sounds go higher and where they go lower (Example 9)

EXAMPLE 9 "Bounce High"

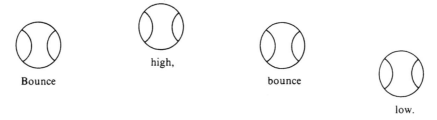

Many young children have real difficulty with such simple tasks as learning to hold a pencil correctly, printing their names, and trying to print on lines or to form letters correctly. The first-grade teacher should not add pencil-and-paper music writing to those problems.

The beginning of second grade is a good time to introduce actual music manuscript. The first music writing should relate very directly to the symbolic sound representations the children used in earlier lessons—hearts for beats, rosies and balls and teddy bears for notes. The shift to standard notation can be made quickly enough once the children appear ready.

When actual notation is begun, attention must be paid to size and spacing of notes. Such things as slant should be pointed out and corrected. Much board notation should be done, both by teacher and by children. It should go without saying that the teacher's music writing must be exemplary—a model for children's.

For each new note introduced—for each new rhythm—there should be writing papers for the class. However, music writing takes a great deal of time if one expects children to notate complete songs.

The author struggled with this problem for a number of years and finally came to the conclusion, after trying several different approaches to music writing, that it wasn't so much the amount of music writing that mattered as the frequency with which children notate. Short experiences, given often, seemed to do far more for developing notational skill than writing whole songs occasionally. Give the children familiar songs completely notated except for a bar or two or, sometimes, a phrase left out. If the song is in *aaba* form, leave out one of the *a* phrases; that way, the children have in the other *a* phrases a model for placing, spacing, and shaping the notes they write.

If the children just learned a new rhythmic figure——give them a notated song from which all but one of the 's have been left out. The one is a model for their notation.

Sometimes, part of a lesson must be spent on some specific aspect of notation. One must teach that

1. Stems should be as long as from the second line to just above the fourth line of the staff.

2. Note placement should relate to beats (four sixteenth notes or two eighth notes should occupy the space of one quarter note). This is not so much said as constantly shown.

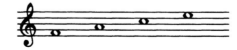

3. Noteheads in spaces have to fill the space; that is, they must touch the line above and the line below.

4. Noteheads on lines have to be half above and half below the line and must be the same size as the noteheads in spaces.

5. Stems go on the right side of notes (not out of the middle like lollipops).

6. Draw noteheads first, then stems.

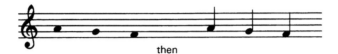

7. The third line is the middle of the staff. Below it, stems go up and on the right side of the note; above it, stems go down and on the left side of the note.

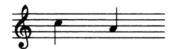

8. When eighth notes are on the same line or in the same space, the bridge is straight.

When they are on different lines or spaces, the stems should be drawn first, of the correct size, and then the bridge to connect them.

Each of these ideas should be presented in a different lesson—in a writing lesson focused on that single aspect.

Just as children need practice to form letters correctly, they need practice to form notes correctly and to place them on the staff in such a way that they can be read by others.

With older children, a good inducement to music writing is the opportunity to compose: "For homework compose a four-phrase rhythm in § in *abba* form." Give them a form within which to notate and suggestions as to the rhythmic patterns that can be used (see Example 10). To the extent that children can write music, they will be able to read music. The two skills go hand-in-hand.

EXAMPLE 10

Music Reading

Any time the eye helps the voice, music reading is taking place. From the time the child follows the teacher's hand levels when learning a new song, he or she is reading—interpreting the hand in a higher place to mean a higher sound, the hand in a lower place to mean a lower sound. The process of transferring this to notation on a printed page is slow, systematic, and specific.

From reading flash cards in first grade to reading songs in third and fourth grades to following a theme in a score in fifth and sixth grades, the principles are the same. And they may be established early through the reading of flash cards that show rhythm patterns taken from familiar songs.

Each card should contain a four-beat pattern.[3] For example:

The teacher shows a card briefly, saying rhythmically, "One, two, ready, read!" On the word *read,* the card should be out of sight so that children are encouraged to think and recall by pattern rather than to read note-by-note. This is similar to linguistic reading in which children are encouraged to read phrases and sentences rather than individual letters or words.

The first reading of whole songs could occur early in grade two: The children follow with pointing finger the notation of songs already known well, singing them first in *ti-ta*'s, then in solfa, and then with words. The teacher must monitor these experiences carefully to make sure that the children are pointing to what they are singing. More than one child has been known to look at the wrong line, or even the wrong song.

The preparation for "reading" these known songs must be no less thorough because they are known.

Children should be prepared for following staff notation using a "flying note" on a board staff:

[3]Four-beat patterns are used because they conform to the usual phrase length of children's songs.

The teacher can take the children through the intervals and melodic turns they will encounter in the song to be "read."

For reading something the children have not seen or heard before, the preparation must be even more thorough. Place the rhythm on the board and use it as a rhythm-erase exercise, having the children (1) identify its meter, (2) read its rhythm, (3) analyze its form for like and unlike phrases, and (4) memorize it. Then erase it, either a phrase at a time or in its entirety, and have them reconstruct it on the board or on papers. They have then "read" the rhythm of the new song, although they don't yet realize it. They have also derived the form and determined the meter.

Next, prepare the tone set or scale for them, using the flying note to drill the melodic vocabulary—the turns and intervals in the song in the key in which it will be read. This is much in the way a reading teacher presents new words to a class before asking them to read a story containing them.

If one goes through these steps conscientiously in grades two, three, and four, students will probably begin to assume some of the preparation tasks themselves by the end of the fourth grade. Still, some teacher guidance is necessary. When the students look at a new song (Example 11, for instance), the teacher should ask the following questions:

"What meter are we in?" [$\frac{4}{4}$]

"Look through the rhythm. Are there any measures we need to practice before we read?"

"Let's read the rhythm." Then: "One, two, ready, read."

"Look at the key signature. One flat? Where is *do*?" [on F]

"What note does the song end on? F (*do*) or D (*la*)?"

"Is it in major or minor?" [major]

EXAMPLE 11   "Rattlesnake"

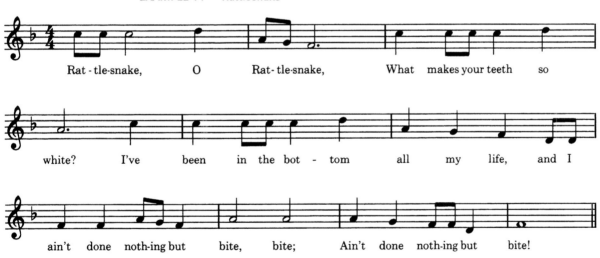

At this point, the tone set must be constructed on the board and the intervals and melodic turns needed for reading practiced.

"Read the first phrase to yourself." [Inner hearing. Teacher gives starting pitch and tempo and may keep an audible beat.]

"Now aloud."

(The phrase is sung aloud, first by the group and then by several individual children.)

"Are any other phrases the same? Sing those."
"Look at the *b (c)* phrase. Sing it to yourself."
"Now aloud together."

(These phrases are sung by the group, then by individual children, and then again by the group.)

"Now the whole song."

At this point, it will probably be sung through by the class correctly in solfa, and the teacher may think the job is done. It isn't! The step from solfa to words isn't a step, it's a leap.

The next step is to take away the solfa and sing on a neutral syllable. At this stage, musical mistakes will happen. Return to solfa and correct them. When the tune can be sung correctly on "loo," add the words.

CONCLUSION

Children do not learn to read the language they speak in one year. By sixth grade, they are still barely able to read a newspaper in many instances—after speaking their language for ten years and after six years of daily reading lessons, with additional reading practice in every other subject they study. Can children really be expected to read music when they have lessons perhaps only twice weekly?

The expectation that they read music is not unrealistic, but the level of expectation is usually far too high, and the help and preparation for reading within the lesson is usually far too little.

- Give children easier reading experiences.
- Give reading experiences more often; reading one phrase every lesson will do more good than reading a whole song once a month.
- Help the children by separating out and solving the reading hurdles before they occur.
- Keep the reading examples a full level or more below the rote experiences.

Above all, if the teacher can build in students a desire to read and write music, then whatever musical learning is achieved in the music class will probably be carried into out-of-school life. People tend to learn those things they really want to learn.

ACTIVITIES

1. Construct a set of rhythm flash cards for use with a second-grade class. Practice using them with your classmates.

2. Pick a song for a music-reading experience for a third-grade class. Write a detailed lesson for presenting it.

CHAPTER 7

ACTIVITIES THROUGH WHICH CHILDREN LEARN MUSIC
Listening

HEARING VERSUS LISTENING

Hearing and listening are not the same thing. Anyone with normally functioning ears hears all sounds occurring in the immediate environment. The extent to which those sounds are consciously registered depends almost entirely upon whether the individual is listening or simply "hearing." The ears may dismiss such sounds as distant traffic noise, the clacking of office equipment, telephones ringing in other peoples' offices, and shopping mall or elevator music. The mind tends to ignore sound that cannot be controlled and that has no implications for the "hearer." From birth, people are increasingly conditioned to "tune out" irrelevant sound—sound they hear but to which there is no need to listen. This largely twentieth-century lesson of tuning out is learned well, and it is learned young. By the time children come to school, many of them are past masters at avoiding listening. It has become necessary for the school to teach children to distinguish between "hearing" and "listening" and to teach children when and how to listen.

LEARNING TO LISTEN

Focusing on listening in a musical context is simply one part of focusing on the general skill of listening in the primary grades. Most children will be more likely to be able to listen to music if they also know how to listen to a story or to a set of simple verbal directions.

To that end, here are some techniques to encourage attentive listening.

1. Use silence effectively. Teachers, especially beginning teachers, often seem to have a compulsion to fill any silence with words. If a child does not immediately answer a teacher's question, the teacher should wait, resisting the impulse to rush in with the answer, showing a patient and supportive listening attitude. This is a "modeling" behavior for listening. It encourages the rest of the

class to listen, also—and, incidentally, it is surprising how many children can come up with a "right" answer given a few more moments in which to think.

2. Say things only once. If the teacher as a matter of habit repeats every direction two or three times, children quickly realize it isn't necessary to "listen" the first time.

3. Ask to see children's eyes before giving directions. Establishing eye contact is a way of ensuring that the ears are engaged.

4. At beginning stages, give only one direction at a time. Do not say,

"Fold your paper lengthwise, number it from one to ten, and put your name on the top."

Do say,

"Fold your paper this way." (wait)
"Number it from one to ten." (wait)
"Put your name on the top."

Later, children will be able to listen with comprehension to directions involving several steps, but that is a learned skill.

5. Make a general rule for classroom discussions that when one person is speaking, others must be quiet. (This will not ensure that they are listening, but it will make it possible for them to do so.)

6. Use positive reinforcement: "I like the way Susan and John are ready to listen."

The following are some activities that can be used to reinforce listening skills.

1. Read part of a story to the children at a regular time every day, a time designated as "Listening Time." Set a listening mood for the story. Continue the story over more than one lesson. Guide listening by asking questions:

"What happened to the gray fox yesterday?"
"How do you suppose he is going to escape?"
"Let's listen to find out."

2. Have the children close their eyes for one minute (this eliminates visual distractions) and listen to discover how many different environmental sounds they can identify in that time. List the sounds on the chalkboard (a truck passing, someone walking down the hall, someone sneezing, the heat fans going on, and so on).

3. Give as homework: "Collect all the sounds you hear on the way home. Write them down. Be ready to share your list with the class tomorrow."

Such activities are geared simply to make children aware of the world of sound and of the difference between being in the presence of sound—*hearing*—and being totally conscious of that sound—*listening*.

LISTENING TO MUSIC

Activities for developing music-listening skills should be interspersed with those aimed at general listening skills. Since not all children are particularly verbal, it may well be that some who cannot listen quietly and with understanding to a story will listen quietly and with visible enjoyment to music.

Certainly, the best early music-listening experiences for kindergarten and first-grade children are those in which the teacher sings to them—lullabies, story songs, holiday songs, songs about the rain or snow. There is absolutely no more effective way to encourage listening than the direct oral transmission of the musical experience from performer to listener.

It matters little if the teacher's voice is not beautiful—or even if the tune isn't always accurate. If children like the teacher, they will like the teacher's singing. In any case, too much has been made of the "beautiful" voice in teaching. A song sung with expressiveness and obvious enjoyment will mean far more to children than one sung more musically correctly but coldly.

The *listening song* should be scheduled for its moment in the day like the story hour. Like the "story," the listening song should be prepared by some general motivational discussion and by guide questions:

"How many of you have a dog?"
"The man in this song had a special kind of dog. Listen to see what kind of dog he had and what wonderful things the dog did."

The same listening song may be repeated many times during the year. Indeed, if it is not, children will probably request it. Just as children love to have the same bedtime story read *ad infinitum,* until they can almost recite it word-for-word, so also do they want to hear the same listening songs again and again if those songs were well chosen. A core of five or six good listening songs is probably enough for one school year.

OTHER MUSIC FOR LISTENING

Although songs sung by the teacher should be among the first listening experiences, they need not be the only music-listening experiences for the kindergarten and first-grade child. When children are exhibiting good listening skills, the teacher may substitute an easy, singable theme from a masterwork—for example, the Romanze from *Eine kleine Nachtmusik* by Mozart—humming, or singing the melody on a neutral syllable. After a few hearings of the tune performed in this way, the children will be as familiar with the melody as with their listening songs or their favorite stories. At this point, the teacher may play a record or a tape of the work for the children and then place it at the *listening station* so that individual children may listen to it when they wish.

THE LISTENING STATION

In every classroom, there should be a table set up for listening, with a good quality tape player and earphones. Children should be free to go to this table when other work is completed or at times during the day when there may be free-choice activities. A "library" of carefully chosen tapes should be available on the table. These may include some story tapes, but they should also include some music without dialogue. Much of the material commercially available for children's listening surrounds and overlays the music with childish rather than childlike stories in which instruments speak and have personalities. This sort of "talking down" to children is both needless and counterproductive. The focus of these recordings is not the music but the story. Indeed, such music as is on them is often of very questionable quality. What the children remember is the story, not the music.

Far better story tapes may be found by searching out those drawn from children's literature. Far better music-listening experiences will occur if the music tapes are just that—music.

The purpose of the classroom listening station is not entertainment but education. That education can and should be enjoyable, but the materials used for it should have intrinsic value as literature or music. There is more than enough entertainment available to children in after-school hours.

A SCHOOLWIDE LISTENING STRATEGY

People tend to like best what they know best. The unfamiliar and new is often greeted with, if not dislike, at least distrust. The radio vendors of popular music are well aware of this fact and, therefore, see to it that certain new recordings are played many times over relatively short time spans, so that the listening public cannot fail to know (and buy) them. Taste and choice are in this way very consciously manipulated by the industry.

The lessons to be learned from this are that

1. People like what they know.
2. Something heard five times is more likely to be "known" and "liked" than something heard once.
3. The strategy employed to sell popular music can also be employed, albeit on a smaller scale, to sell serious music.

In a day of mass communication, when nearly every household has radios, tape decks, record and compact disc players, television sets and VCR machines, all largely devoted to the perpetuation of popular music, the future of serious music could be ensured if only a small part of each school day were to be devoted to it. With that in mind, two British Columbia teachers, Karen E. Taylor and David Brummitt,[1] have developed a series of listening lessons and a "script" to be used over schoolwide speaker systems daily.

Everything in the school comes to a standstill during the "listening time." Teachers do not put on board work or mark papers. Desks are clear of any distractions. Everyone in the school stops everything and *listens*. One composition is repeated for five successive days, and a different but repetitive script is supplied to be read before each listening. The script comes with pronunciation guides, and the listening example takes no more than six minutes daily. School participation in the project is voluntary, but twenty-nine out of thirty-two schools have opted to participate. Although, unfortunately, no "before-and-after" testing has been done to document the effectiveness of the project, anecdotal records have been kept of children's and parents' responses to it. The participants have no doubt as to its impact.

Three examples of one week's script are shown on pages 75–77.[2]

Each participating school has been required to purchase the needed tapes and to send the expected "narrator" to workshops at which the compositions are introduced and studied.

The authors of this series of listening experiences expect to have a three-year cycle of lessons by the time the work is completed.

[1]Langley, B. C., School District #35.
[2]Used by permission of the authors.

September 14–18 (Week 2)

Composer: Wolfgang Amadeus Mozart   **Time:**   6′
              (1756–1791)

Composition: *Eine kleine Nachtmusik,* Serenade in Gm, K. 525 (first
                  movement)

Outstanding Features:

    Rhythm:
    Melody: Singable theme
    Harmony:
    Form:
    Tempo: Allegro
    Timbre: String orchestra
    Dynamics:
    Style:

Performance: Vienna Philharmonic Orchestra, Karl Bohm

Recording: DG 413 152-4 GW

Day 1: This week's feature composer is Wolfgang Amadeus Mozart. The feature composition is *Eine kleine Nachtmusik* (I'na Kly' na Nocht' moo zeek). The title of this composition is in German because that is the language Mozart spoke. In English, *Eine kleine Nachtmusik* means "A Little Nightmusic."

Day 2: This week's feature composer is Wolfgang Amadeus Mozart. The feature composition is *Eine kleine Nachtmusik* (I'na Kly' na Nocht' moo zeek). Mozart composed *Eine kleine Nachtmusik* ("A Little Nightmusic") for people to listen to after a fancy dinner. This is how wealthy people and kings and queens entertained themselves about 200 years ago.

Day 3: This week's feature composer is Wolfgang Amadeus Mozart. The feature composition is *Eine keine Nachtmusik* (I'na Kly' na Nocht' moo zeek). Mozart composed *Eine keine Nachtmusik* ("A Little Nightmusic") for an orchestra of stringed instruments—violin, viola, cello, and double bass. An orchestra made up of these instruments is called a string orchestra.

Day 4: This week's feature composer is Wolfgang Amadeus Mozart. The feature composition is *Eine kleine Nachtmusik* (I'na Kly' na Nocht' moo zeek). Do you remember the group of instruments for which Mozart composed *Eine kleine Nachtmusik*? (Short pause). If you are thinking of string orchestra—violin, viola, cello, and double bass—you are correct.

Day 5: This week's feature composition is *Eine kleine Nachtmusik*. Do you remember the name of the composer of *Eine kleine Nachtmusik*? (Short pause). If you are thinking of Wolfgang Amadeus Mozart, you are right.

September 21–25 (Week 3)

Composer: Antonio Vivaldi (1678–1741)   Time: 5'

Composition: "Autumn" from *The Four Seasons*
Concerto in E, Op. 8, No. 1, R. 269

Outstanding Features:
Rhythm:
Harmony: Unison/solo
Form: ABA$_{vi}$B$_v$A$_{vii}$CA
Timbre: Harpsichord/string orchestra/solo violin
Dynamics: Loud/soft
Style: Program music (Vivaldi composed sonnets for each movement of the four concertos *The Four Seasons*)

Performance: Violin, Jose-Luis Garcia
English Chamber Orchestra, Leonard Slatkin

Recording: RCA HRE1-5827

Day 1: This week's feature composer is Antonio Vivaldi. The feature composition is "Autumn" from *The Four Seasons*. This is the week of the Autumn equinox, September 21 (or 2__), which marks the first day of Autumn. People have celebrated the beginning of Autumn for centuries. Vivaldi, a musician who lived 250 years ago, was very sensitive to the changing seasons. He described Autumn in two ways. In words, he said, "Dancing and singing celebrate the joys of a good harvest." In music, he wrote the composition "Autumn."

Day 2: This week's feature composer is Antonio Vivaldi. The feature composition is "Autumn" from the *The Four Seasons*. "Dancing and singing celebrate the joys of a good harvest." Vivaldi composed Autumn for string orchestra, and he thought these instruments expressed his words very well. Vivaldi chose one instrument of the string orchestra, the violin, to sometimes play by itself. The violin leads the other instruments in "dancing and singing [to] celebrate the joys of a good harvest."

Day 3: This week's feature composer is Antonio Vivaldi. The feature composition is "Autumn" from the *The Four Seasons*. Vivaldi chose one instrument to lead the other instruments of the string orchestra in celebrating Autumn. Do you remember the name of that instrument? (Short pause). It is the violin. The other instruments in the string orchestra are viola, cello, and double bass.

Day 4: This week's feature composer is Antonio Vivaldi. The feature composition is "Autumn" from the *The Four Seasons*. Vivaldi described Autumn in two ways. In words, he said, "Dancing and singing celebrate the joys of a good harvest." In music, he chose instruments to speak for him. Do you remember what they were? (Short pause). If you are thinking of the violin, viola, cello, and double bass you are correct. Or maybe you are thinking of the string orchestra. You are correct, too.

Day 5: This week's feature composition is "Autumn" from the *The Four Seasons*. Can you think of the name of the composer? (Short pause). Did you think of Vivaldi? That is right. Vivaldi was a musician who was sensitive to the changing of the seasons. He composed this music to celebrate the Autumn season. Perhaps we will hear from Vivaldi again. (Note to teacher: See January, Week 1.)

October 26–30 (Week 4)

Composer: Modest Mussorgsky   **Time:** 3'45" (piano)
                                                                3'30" (orch.)
Composition: *Pictures at an Exhibition*   (synth.)

                  "Promenade" and "The Gnome"

Outstanding Features:
    Timbre: Piano, orchestra, synthesizer
    Style: Program music

Performance: Vladimir Ashkenazy, piano
                  Los Angeles Philharmonic, Zubin Mehta

Recording: London CS5-6559
                  (contains original piano version and Ravel's transcription for
                  orchestra)

Day 1: This week's feature composer is Modest Mussorgsky (Mu zor' ski). The
feature composition is *Pictures at an Exhibition*. Composers get musical
ideas in different ways. Mussorgsky got the idea for this composition in a
special way. He had a friend who was an artist. His friend died. After his
death, Mussorgsky went to an exhibition of his friend's paintings.
Mussorgsky wanted this composition to tell about his walk in the art
gallery and the paintings he saw. He went home to his piano and composed *Pictures at an Exhibition*.

Day 2: This week's feature composer is Modest Mussorgsky (Mu zor' ski). The
feature composition is *Pictures at an Exhibition*. Mussorgsky wanted *Pictures at an Exhibition* to tell about his walk in the art gallery and the paintings he saw. The pictures were special to him because they had been
painted by his friend who had died. The opening theme is Mussorgsky as
he moved from one picture to another. The next section is to describe the
first painting which shows a small Gnome with crooked legs whose
movements are strange and are accompanied by savage shrieks.

Day 3: This week's feature composer is Modest Mussorgsky (Mu zor' ski). The
feature composition is *Pictures at an Exhibition*. Another musician,
Maurice Ravel, heard Mussorgsky's music. He could almost see the same
pictures as Mussorgsky but he made the music tell about them in a different way. Ravel used the instruments of the orchestra to help us see the
Pictures at an Exhibition.

Day 4: This week's feature composer is Modest Mussorgsky (Mu zor' ski). The
feature composition is *Pictures at an Exhibition*. Ravel used the instruments of the orchestra to help us see the pictures Mussorgsky composed
for the piano. The opening theme is Mussorgsky as he moved from one
picture to another. Next, Mussorgsky wrote music to describe the first
painting, which shows a small Gnome with crooked legs whose movements are strange and are accompanied by savage shrieks.

Day 5: This week's feature composition is *Pictures at an Exhibition*. Do you
remember the name of the composer of *Pictures at an Exhibition*? That's
right. It was that long name, Mussorgsky. Mussorgsky's music is so descriptive that many musicians get ideas when they hear it. One Japanese
musician, Tomita, used the synthesizer to paint Mussorgsky's pictures.
Even though Tomita used Mussorgsky's music quite precisely, it sounds
very different than either Mussorgsky's original piano compostion or
Ravel's arrangement for orchestra. Do you think Mussorgsky would have
liked Tomita's performance?

DIRECTED AND NONDIRECTED LISTENING

All the listening experiences described thus far have been relatively nondirective. That is, some information may have been supplied before the listening or between repeated listenings, but the student's attention was not directed toward musical characteristics of the compositions being listened to. Children were not directed to listen specifically for certain things.

There is a place in curriculum for both directed and nondirected listening. Indeed, the same composition may be approached at different times in both of these ways. Directed listening, however, requires more musical knowledge of both students and teacher than nondirected.

Directed Listening

In simplest terms, in directed listening the teacher asks the students to listen for specific things. Generally, each lesson focuses on only one aspect of the music. During repeated hearings, different characteristics of the music are highlighted through adroit questioning. Children may chart the various things they discover in the music.

Some typical guide questions might be:

"How many times does the first theme (tune) occur?"

"What instrument(s) is (are) playing the theme at each entrance?" Or, if it is a one-instrument piece, "Is the theme being played at a high, middle, or low place at each entrance?"

"Call the first theme *A*. Diagram the form as you listen. What form is the piece?"

"How does the composer use loud and soft (dynamics) to create interest?"

"Does the music get faster or slower (tempo)?" "Gradually or suddenly? At which theme statement?"

"At which theme statement does the music change from minor to major?" (Major to minor?)

"How is the second theme different from the first?" (Major-minor; faster-slower; softer-louder, and so on).

"Is there a place where the theme is done like a round or canon? At which theme statement?"

"Where is the theme twice as fast (diminished)? Twice as slow (augmented)?"

Although some of the preceding questions are not appropriate for some compositions, most work with many compositions. The teacher must listen to the selection a sufficient number of times to know which questions will apply best to it.

CONCLUSION

Listening is a taught skill. The earliest music-listening experiences for young children should be very personal ones—listening to each other, listening to environmental sounds, listening to the teacher sing. Later, listening stations can be employed to advantage. Experiences in listening to tapes and records can be either nondirected ("Listen!") or directed ("Listen to discover what/where/when/ how..."). Whether listening is directed or nondirected, the most important factor in getting children to "like" music selected for listening is the frequency with which that music is played for them.

ACTIVITIES

1. Find six songs that could be used with the first grade for listening. Include a variety of song types. Choose one and present it as you would to the children.

2. Choose five tapes you would place at a listening station for third graders. Tell why you chose each.

3. Select a composition you like. Prepare a plan for a series of directed listening for it for fifth and sixth graders.

The following is a list of thirty-one recordings that should be in every school.[3]

ANGEL

Recording: Angel 4XS 36799
Performance: London Symphony Orchestra, Sir Adrian Boult
Composer: Ralph Vaughan Williams (1872–1958)
Composition: Fantasia on "Greensleeves"

Recording: Angel 4AE 34462
Performance: Otto Klemperer
Composer: Wolfgang Amadeus Mozart (1756–1791)
Composition: Overture to *The Magic Flute*

DEUTSCHE GRAMMOPHON

Recording: 411-720-4 (L 'Oiseau Lyre)
Performance: Academy of Ancient Music, Christopher Hogwood
Composer: Wolfgang Amadeus Mozart (1756–1791)
Composition: *Eine kleine Nachtmusik,* Serenade in G Minor, K. 525

Recording: DG Walkman Classics 413148-4
Performance: Berlin Philharmonic Orchestra, Rafael Kubelik
Composer: George Frideric Handel (1685–1759)
Composition: *Water Music*/Sinfonia from *Messiah*/*Music for the Royal Fireworks*

Recording: Deutsche Grammophon DG 330-201 (Christmas Concertos)
Performance: Berlin Philharmonic, Herbert von Karajan
Composer: Arcangelo Corelli (1653–1713)
Composition: Concerto Grosso in G Minor, Op. 6, No. 8 ("Christmas Concerto")

Recording: DG 3343 502
Performance: Amadeus Quartet
Composer: Franz Joseph Haydn (1732–1809)
Composition: String Quartet in C Major, Op. 76, No. 3 *(Emperor)*

Recording: DG 3335 202
Performance: Berlin Philharmonic, Herbert von Karajan
Composer: Béla Bartók (1881–1945)
Composition: Concerto for Orchestra (second movement)

Recording: DG 410 845-4 GS
Performance: Boston Symphony Orchestra, Seiji Ozawa
Composer: Gustav Mahler (1860–1911)
Composition: Symphony No. 1, in D

[3]While many of these selections are the author's choices, the major work of finding good recordings of them was done by Karen E. Taylor and David Brummitt, the two music educators who developed the *Langley, B.C., Non-Directed Listening Program.*

DEUTSCHE GRAMMOPHON *(cont.)*

Recording: DG 3302 083
Performance: Los Angeles Philharmonic Orchestra, Leonard Bernstein
Composer: Aaron Copland (b. 1900)
Composition: *Appalachian Spring*

Recording: DG 3301 106
Performance: Berlin Philharmonic, Herbert von Karajan
Composer: Ludwig van Beethoven (1770–1827)
Composition: Symphony No. 6 (fifth movement, after introduction)

EMI ANGEL

Recording: EMI Angel 4XS-37846
Performance: Sviatoslav Richter, piano, and members of the Borodin Quartet
Composer: Franz Schubert (1797–1828)
Composition: Piano Quintet in A Major *(The Trout)*

LONDON

Recording: London CS56559
Performance: Vladimir Ashkenazy, piano; Los Angeles Philharmonic, Zubin
                Mehta
Composer: Mussorgsky/Ravel
Composition: *Pictures at an Exhibition* (piano and transcription for orchestra)

Recording: London 41711 44
Performance: London Sinfonietta, Riccardo Chailly
Composer: Igor Stravinsky (1882–1971)
Composition: Octet for Winds

PHILIPS

Recording: Philips 7311 080
Performance: I Musici
Composer: Antonio Vivaldi (1678–1741)
Composition: Flute Concerto in F

Recording: Philips 7310 085
Performance: I Musici
Composer: Tomaso Albinoni (1671–1750)
Composition: Concerto in F for Two Oboes, Op. 9, No. 3/Adagio in G Minor for Strings
                and Organ

Recording: Philips 411-134-4
Performance: Academy of St. Martin-in-the-Fields, Neville Marriner
Composer: Wolfgang Amadeus Mozart (1756–1791)
Composition: Sinfonia Concertante in E-flat/Oboe Concerto

Recording: Philips 412 737-4 PH
Performance: Hermann Baumann, horn; St. Paul Chamber Orchestra, Pinchas
                Zukerman
Composer: Wolfgang Amadeus Mozart (1756–1791)
Composition: Horn Concerto in D (second movement, Allegro), K. 514

Recording: Philips 412 216-4
Performance: Leipzig Gewandhaus Orchestra, Kurt Masur
Composer: Johannes Brahms (1833–1897)
Composition: Symphony No. 1

RCA

Recording: RCA HRE 1-5827
Performance: Violin, Jose-Luis Garcia; English Chamber Orchestra, Leonard
                Slatkin
Composer: Antonio Vivaldi (1678–1741)
Composition: *The Four Seasons*

Recording: RCA ARK 1-3437
Performance: Vienna Boys Choir
Composer: Benjamin Britten (1913–1976)
Composition: *A Ceremony of Carols*

RCA *(cont.)*

Recording: RCA ARK 1-0838
Performance: Tomita on Synthesizer
Composer: Modest Mussorgsky
Composition: *Pictures at an Exhibition*

SERAPHIM

Recording: Seraphim 4XG-60235
Performance: Leopold Stokowski
Composer: Johann Sebastian Bach (1685–1750)
Composition: Little Fugue in G Minor (orchestral transcription)

CBS

Recording: CBS MT 35134
Performance: Murray Perahia, piano; the English Chamber Orchestra
Composer: Wolfgang Amadeus Mozart (1756–1791)
Composition: Piano Concerto No. 20

Recording: CBS FMT 3940—A Canadian Brass Christmas
Performance: The Canadian Brass
Composition: Various Christmas carols

Recording: CBS Records Masterworks-MPT 38786
Performance: Harold Wright, clarinet
Composer: Wolfgang Amadeus Mozart (1756–1791)
Composition: Quintet for Clarinet and Strings in A, K. 581

Recording: CBS MT 31840—Best of Bach
Performance: E. Power Biggs
Composer: Johann Sebastian Bach (1685–1750)
Composition: Little Fugue in G minor

Recording: CBS MYT 37766
Performance: New York Philharmonic, Leonard Bernstein
Composer: Peter Ilyich Tchaikovsky
Composition: Symphony No. 4

Recording: CBS MT 39310
Performance: Winton Marsalis
Composer: Franz Joseph Haydn (1732–1809)
Composition: Trumpet Concerto in E-flat (third movement)

COLUMBIA

Recording: Columbia Masterworks MT-35853 1979
Performance: Liona Boyd and the English Chamber Orchestra
Composer: Johann Sebastian Bach/Tomaso Albinoni
Composition: "Jesu, Joy of Man's Desiring"/Adagio for Strings

OTHER

Recording: A Garden of Bell
Performance: Vancouver Chamber Choir
Composer: R. Murray Schafer
Composition: *Gamelan*

Recording: MMG CMG 1105—The King's Singers Madrigal Collection
Performance: The King's Singers
Composer: Thomas Morley
Composition: "Now Is the Month of Maying"

There are also two extensive listening series that may be in schools or school systems: RCA Victor Adventures in Music and Bowmar Listening Library.

In addition, most school series books include some listening examples for each grade and supply listening guides for them.

ACTIVITIES THROUGH WHICH CHILDREN LEARN MUSIC
Creating

"Create!"

The very word strikes terror into the hearts of many teachers. After all, one must be a genius to "create." Something wonderful and mystic happens, and from out of nowhere except the mind of the artist, writer, or composer pops a newly created work of art.

Not so!

New art, new literature, new music is not invented out of whole cloth but is the result of an artist's reacting to many previous experiences and organizing those experiences into something "new." The richer the past experiences, the more the artist has to draw on in "creating." Bach was born into a family for whom music was a daily experience. Mozart's father was a professional musician. Both these composers possessed musical genius, but both also had a wealth of musical experience on which to draw, even as children. Nothing was ever created in a vacuum.

CREATING AS ORGANIZING

One need not be a Bach or a Mozart to create something in music. Given sufficient guidance, any child can organize what he or she knows into something "new"—can improvise or compose—can create. The music curriculum that does not provide opportunities for children to do this is neglecting perhaps the most important of musical skills. Through creating, all the other skills—singing, moving, playing, reading, writing, and listening—may be brought together meaningfully. Through creating, the elements of music—melody, rhythm, form, harmony, tempo, dynamics, and timbre—may each, in turn, be studied and combined in various ways. The *organization of sound,* the act of *creating music,* is the synthesis of musical experience and knowledge and can be a center around which all other musical learning revolves.

Creative activities in classroom music may be separated roughly into six areas: text, rhythm, melody, form, harmony, and expressive elements (tempo, dynamics, and timbre).

CREATING TEXT

Even the youngest children love supplying new words for a song. Initially, the teacher should ask for no more than one or two new words—although when children supply more, their contributions should, of course, be accepted (see Example 1). Later, when children are working on rhyming words in language, they can use this skill to create new phrases or verses in songs. For example, the original song "Phoebe" (Example 2) may become

Jimmy in his underwear,
Jimmy in his hat,
Jimmy in his underwear,
. . . .

(Playing with the cat.)
(What do you think of that!)
(Standing on a mat.)
(Chasing round a rat.)
Etc.

or

Jamie in a bright red dress,
Jamie in her shoes,
Jamie in a bright red dress,
. . . .

(Gee, I wonder, whose?)
(Bringing us the news.)
Etc.

or

Johnny in his socks,
Sitting on the rocks.

or

Mary in her coat,
Rowing in a boat.

EXAMPLE 1

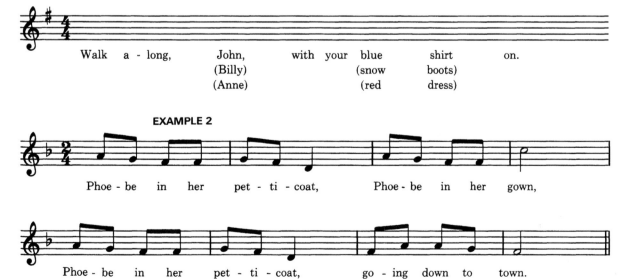

EXAMPLE 2

With practice, children can become highly inventive at changing existing texts. It is something they have done for generations in their own play—not always with results adults would wish to hear.

When children are able to sense phrase and meter in rhyme—that is, how many syllables are needed to "fill" a phrase—they may be able to create entire new verses for known songs. These verses can extend a story or can be totally unrelated to the original song.

New Text to Extend a Story

EXAMPLE 3

In Example 3, only the middle section need be changed to create a whole new story:

> . . . and all the insects came to bake
> some cookies and a wedding cake.
>
> . . . the bride flew east and the groom flew west,
> then both flew over the robin's nest.
>
> . . . the robin looked up and swallowed the groom,
> the bee flew back to her own little room.

The story has been extended by some classes to indicate in great detail who came to the wedding. No two classes are likely to end the song in precisely the same way.

When the teacher is soliciting lines for the song from children, he or she should accept incomplete lines. What one child begins, often another can complete. It may also happen that a day or a week later, a child will bring a complete new verse to add. Once turned to this kind of task, children's minds do not leave it simply because the music period, or the school day, is over.

New Text Unrelated to the Original

Sometimes, children enjoy taking a tune they know and putting new words to it for a holiday, for an upcoming event, for a school celebration, or just for fun. They may change a standard text to make it suit the time of year or the familiar surroundings of the area in which they live.

The Texas "rainy day" song shown in Example 4 was changed by Canadian second graders to

Wind is blowing,
Snow is snowing,
Frosty day here to stay,
Fall is going.

EXAMPLE 4

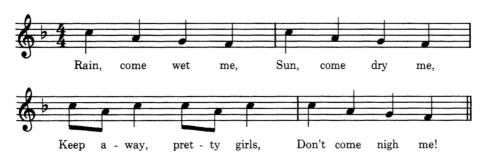

Rain, come wet me, Sun, come dry me,

Keep a - way, pret - ty girls, Don't come nigh me!

Caribbean children sing "Here we go 'round the mango tree" rather than "the mulberry bush." A Caribbean game song, "Four White Horses," became "Four Brown Caribou in the Arctic," as played by children in the Northwest Territories.

Any holiday can provide an opportunity for the creation of text. As Halloween approaches, for example, the teacher could elicit from the children examples of words they associate with that holiday—witches, ghosts, bat, cat, night, black, fright, scare, broomsticks—and then have them find and list rhyming words wherever possible:

    witches—ditches, britches . . .
    ghost(s)—host(s), most, roast . . .
    cat—bat, sat, rat, fat . . .
    black—sack, clack, tack . . .
    fright—might, light, kite, night, sight . . .
    scare—hair, rare, tear, dare . . .
    (broom)stick—lick, tick, kick . . .
    Hallo(ween)—seen, bean, mean . . .

Using a well-known melody and the suggested words and rhyming words, the children can create a new "Halloween song." "Canoe Song" (Example 5) may become

Witches on broomsticks fly
  My what a fright__!
Black cats and goblins cry,
  Halloween night!
Skeletons rattle by,
  Clouds hide the moonlight,
Ghosts sound their mournful sigh,
  Halloween night!

EXAMPLE 5

My pad - dle's keen and bright, Flash - ing with sil - ver,

Fol - low the wild goose flight, Dip, dip, and swing!

In the process of arranging the text, list all suggested lines on the chalkboard. Often, what one child suggests, another can elaborate. In this way, the "final" text belongs to the whole class. This sort of "communal creativity" is not intended to curtail individual inventiveness but, rather, to give it an impetus. When a class has once gone through such an exercise, children may bring forth further verses independently. A process for creating text has been suggested.

CREATING WITH RHYTHM

Creative activities with rhythm must be separated into two categories—those that require at least minimal knowledge of rhythmic notation and those that do not.[1]

Creative Rhythmic Activities That Do Not Require Notation

Body sounds—clapping, stamping, patsching, snapping, clicking—may be used to underline text and to add rhythmic interest to rote songs. Children have been accompanying their own songs and singing games in this way for generations. The complexity of some children's clapping patterns defies adult analysis. The "game" often seems to be to make the patterns increasingly difficult until only two or three children remain who can still perform them. This is likely to happen with or without teacher involvement.

In the classroom, the teacher who can make use of children's natural rhythmic inventiveness and apply it to their "school" music will find that the simplest songs can be more fun to perform. A short repeated rhythmic pattern, called an ostinato, can be created through body sounds and then transferred to rhythm instruments: rhythm sticks, tambourines, triangles, woodblocks, drums. The newly created rhythmic pattern may be played on a "single" instrument to accompany a song or may be "orchestrated" with several instruments playing—at times individually and at other times in ensemble. Appropriate rhythmic introductions and codas may be added.[2]

For example, to accompany the "Curfew Song" (Example 6), one first grader might play an ostinato (Example 7) on woodblock to represent the sound of the big town clock. Another might play Example 8 on sandblocks to represent the shuffling steps of the town crier. Another might play Example 9 on tambourine to illustrate the swinging and rattling of his lantern.

The "introduction" could be a triangle "clock" striking twelve, followed by layered clock sounds, stepping sounds, and lantern sounds, followed by the "clock" striking two.

[1]Although creative movement is one of the most obvious creative rhythmic responses, it has already been discussed in Chapter 4, pp. 39–40, and so will not be further explored here.

[2]The process described here is closely related to the one used in Orff Schulwerk. The teacher interested in further developing a creative rote-rhythmic approach is advised to read Lois Choksy, Robert M. Abramson, Avon Gillespie, and David Woods, *Teaching Music in the Twentieth Century* (Englewood Cliffs, N.J.: Prentice-Hall, 1986), for a full discussion of the Orff approach.

EXAMPLE 6

Hear you peo - ple while I tell you, All the clocks have now struck one, ___

Keep the fire and keep the light, Keep your hous - es safe this night,

Love your God to - night!

EXAMPLE 7

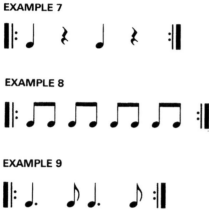

EXAMPLE 8

EXAMPLE 9

It should go without saying that all of this music must be determined by the children, not by the teacher. There is no creativity and little learning involved in such productions if the decisions are the teacher's.

As rhythmic productions like the foregoing one become more complex, children may have difficulty recalling what comes when. The need for a system of encoding becomes apparent; notation becomes a necessity. There is probably no better path to notation than through children's need to retrieve and save their own musical ideas.

However, it should be noted that there are whole societies in which there is no system of musical notation. In these, incredibly complex material is passed in oral transmission from one performer to the next and, indeed, from one generation to the next. Notational skills, while a desirable end of music education in North America, are not necessary for creating.

Creative Rhythmic Activities Using Notation

If children are taught only three symbols—♩ (one sound on one beat), ♪ (one beat of silence), and ♫ (two even sounds over one beat in $\frac{2}{4}$, $\frac{3}{4}$, and $\frac{4}{4}$)—they can begin to notate the simplest rhythmic ostinato patterns they have created. The patterns can be placed by the teacher on charts large enough to be read by the entire group.

From "improvising" rhythms, the children have moved to "composing" rhythms—putting them down in written form so that they will be performed in the same way the next time, and the next.

The earliest "compositions" will probably be only four beats in length, conforming to the phrase length of many songs. By combining various children's four-beat compositions, longer patterns and phrases can be obtained.

It is important when rhythm writing is begun that it always be related immediately back to performance. The child must be able to say, sing, or play what he or she has created. Notation must always be immediately translatable into accurate musical sound.

At this level, the rhythmic vocabulary associated with Kodály practice becomes very useful.[3] With it, children can speak, in accurate rhythm, anything they can notate.

With experience in creating text and rhythm, and with the necessary skills to notate rhythms, children can begin to create and notate rhythms for texts. Often, text determines rhythm and meter to the extent that there appears to be little leeway for creativity:

> *Baa, baa, black sheep,*
> *Have you any wool?*
> *Yes, sir, Yes, sir,*
> *Three bags full!*

would, if noted as spoken by first grader, appear as in Example 10. However, third graders might well experiment with the meter and come up with something like Example 11, whereas fifth graders might use dotted rhythms, as in Example 12, and sixth graders might put it in an asymmetric meter, as in Example 13.

EXAMPLE 10

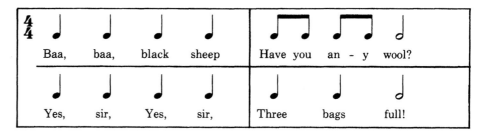

EXAMPLE 11

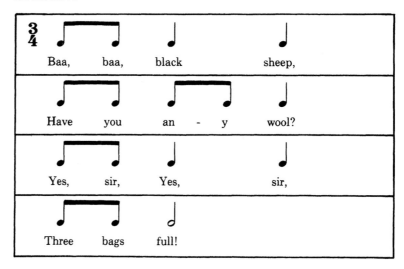

---

[3]*Ta* for ♩, *ti* for ♪ and so on. See Lois Choksy, *The Kodály Method,* 2nd ed. (Englewood Cliffs, N.J.: Prentice-Hall, 1986), pp. 14 and 255, for rhythm syllables as used in Hungary and in North America.

EXAMPLE 12

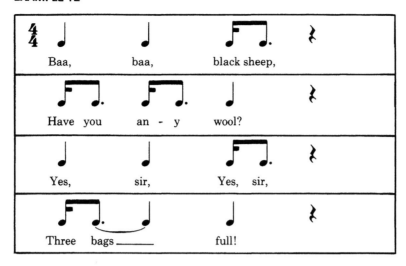

EXAMPLE 13

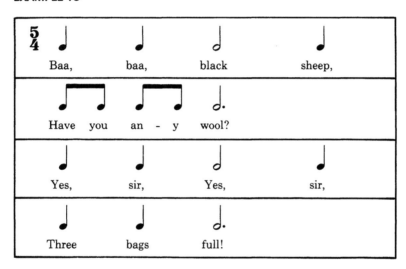

The extent to which children are able to create using rhythm is limited only by the extent of their experience, the level of their skills, and the range of their musical knowledge. All these factors can be, to a large degree, influenced by the school.

CREATING MELODIES

As with all creative endeavor, children's earliest experiments in creating melody rely heavily on imitation. The teacher's melodic question to the kindergarten child (Example 14) will generally result in an answer in the same meter, in a closely related rhythm, and with essentially the same tune (Example 15).

EXAMPLE 14

EXAMPLE 15

It's   snow - ing!

If the teacher asks more open-ended questions, the responses may vary a bit more (Example 16). At this level, answers may be as long or as short as children wish to make them. As long as they are sung, they are correct. Pitch may wander, key may shift, meter may be hard to find. None of that matters. If the child is using melody to relate an event, he or she is "creating." This experience provides the necessary background for later, more specific melodic invention.

EXAMPLE 16

What   did   you   do   last   Sun - day?

In the primary grades, creating texts and improvising and composing rhythms will lead naturally to more balanced melodic improvisations. The teacher can sing a melodic phrase and expect it to be answered with a melodic phrase of the same length (Example 17). Melody will still closely mirror the teacher's in most instances.

EXAMPLE 17

TEACHER

What   did   you   do   last   sum - mer?

CHILD

I   went   to   the   moun - tains.

More inventive melodies begin to occur when the teacher's question ends on a note other than the tonic (I). Example 18 opens a conversation about favorite foods. Because the musical phrase is open, numerous musical answers are possible (Example 19). The children must be made aware of the fact that many different musical answers are both possible and "correct."

From this point, musical "questions" and "answers" should occupy at least some small part of each music period. Further, these need not always be teacher-to-child; they can also be child-to-teacher or child-to-child. This experience gives children freedom with the melodic vocabulary they will need for later, more formal improvisational and compositional activities.

A word should, perhaps, be said here about the use of instruments for melodic improvisation. In some situations, children are encouraged to "create" melodies by dropping mallets randomly on xylophones that have been prepared by the teacher so that they contain only sonorous sounds—a tonic chord or a pentatonic scale, for example.

EXAMPLE 18

Su - sie,   Su - sie,   what   do   you   like   best?

EXAMPLE 19

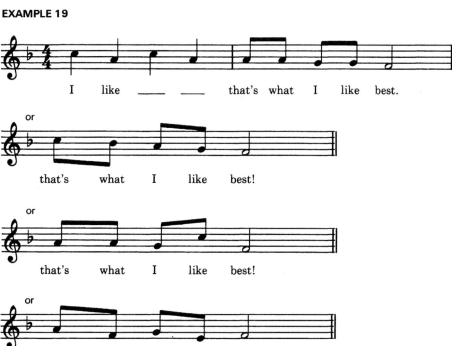

I   like _____ _____   that's   what   I   like   best.

or

that's   what   I   like   best!

or

that's   what   I   like   best!

or

that's   what   I   like   best!

Since the sounds do not exist in the child's mind until after they are produced on the instrument, and since they can rarely be reproduced by the child later with any degree of accuracy, the author considers that such activities produce "accidents" rather than "creations." The fact that some of these accidents may sound good is not enough to elevate them to the level of a creative experience.

That is not to say that instruments cannot be used to create melodies. The child who goes to a keyboard or a barred instrument and thoughtfully picks out a tune, trying numerous possibilities, discarding some, retaining others, and remembering the whole later, has certainly "created" something. The astute teacher will notate this creation for the child. Even if the child cannot read music fluently, he or she will be highly motivated to "read" something self-created.

The composition of complete melodies by upper-grade elementary school children is not an impossibility. Children who have created texts and put those texts in meters and set them to rhythms can also compose melodies for them. Initially, such experiences need to be carefully guided by the teacher.

"Use only the notes C, A, G, F *(s-m-r-d)* in your composition. Make your composition end on *do* (1)."

Such direction makes the task more performable and less threatening to the children. As they acquire security, fewer restrictions need be given, and questions can replace directions:

Do the words make you want to place your melody in major or in minor?

What tonal center (key) will you use?

What scale would you like to use? (pentatonic, diatonic, natural minor, harmonic minor, modal)

How will you use repetition in your melody?

Can you use sequence any place to give your melody more variety?

Children who are asked to improvise and compose melodies regularly do not find the task any more intimidating than the task of using the words in their spelling lessons to make up sentences. The skills involved are essentially the same—using the known vocabulary in a way that is one's own.

CREATING WITHIN FORM

It is through form that all elements are brought together and simple phrases become compositions. Using the idea that in music, some parts should be the same, some similar, and some different, children can create both rhythmic and melodic compositions within forms.

At the simplest level, children may work in pairs. Each child composes a four-beat rhythm pattern. Working together, each pair places its rhythms in a typical song-form pattern: *aabb, aaba,* or *abab.* The rhythms in Example 20 are arranged in *aaba* form and notated in boxes as shown in Example 21. The two children can perform their "rhythm composition" for the class.

Four children working together can compose a "rhythm rondo," deciding together on a pattern for the *a* and each contributing a different pattern for *b, c,* and *d* (Example 22).

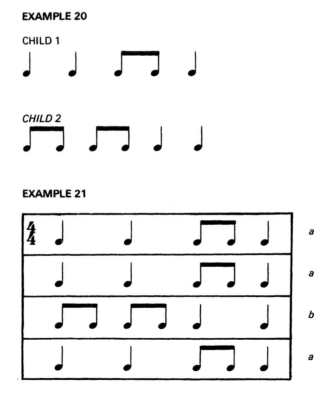

EXAMPLE 20

CHILD 1

CHILD 2

EXAMPLE 21

EXAMPLE 22

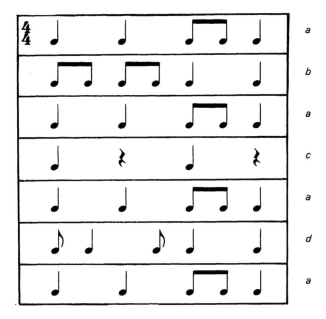

When composing rhythms within forms has become easy, the children may add melodies to the rhythms.

"Use G, F, E, D, C, *(s-f-m-r-d)* for your *a* phrases. Use A, G, and E *(l-s-m)* for your *b* phrase."

Later still, in *aaba* form:

"Make your first *a* phrase a question phrase. End it on *re* or *so* (5). Make your other *a* phrases answers; end them on *do* (1)."

In focusing children's attention in turn on text, rhythm, melody, and form, the teacher is merely isolating those aspects all composers must consider, and by dealing with each aspect separately, children "become" composers at their own level. The musical understandings that result from such composing far outweigh the value of the compositions themselves.

CREATING HARMONY

Two or more musical ideas may occur at the same time. At the lowest level, this happens when the children sing "Ring around the Rosy" and clap Example 23 as an ostinato.

EXAMPLE 23

By second or third grade, when the children are singing securely, melodic ostinati may be introduced. Initially, the teacher should choose and present these, but after experiencing several, children should be able to create their own. This can be most easily done by simply taking a part of the song and using it as an ostinato—

for example, using "Sailing East, Sailing West" (Example 24) against the verse of "Turn the Glasses Over" (Example 25)—or by using a phrase of one song as an ostinato with a second song—"I See the Moon" (Example 26) with "Sally Go 'Round the Sun" (Example 27). Here, the meter of "I See the Moon" was changed from $\frac{2}{4}$ to $\frac{6}{8}$ to make the two songs fit.

Tonal center or keynote can also be used as an ostinato (Example 28).

EXAMPLE 24

Sail - ing   east,   sail - ing   west.

EXAMPLE 25

I've   been   to   Haar - lem,   I've   been   to   Do - ver.

EXAMPLE 26

I   see   the   moon _____

EXAMPLE 27

Sal - ly   go 'round   the   sun, _____   Sal - ly   go 'round   the   moon, _____

Sal - ly   go 'round   the   chim - ney   pot,   ev' - ry   af - ter - noon. _____

EXAMPLE 28

Sal - ly,   Sal - ly

Still later, second parts for songs can be improvised using *do* (1) and *so* (5) to illustrate the harmonic changes implied by the melody. Children sense the right places for change very easily. Later, words can be substituted for *do* (1) and *so* (5), and these harmonizations can also be played on barred instruments (Example 29).

EXAMPLE 29

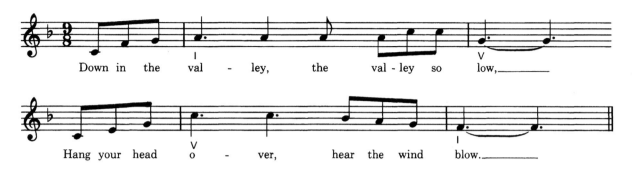

Building triads (1-3-5) over *do* and *so*, the children can construct chords and play their accompaniments for their own melodies. These need not be notated. They can simply be shown by chord symbol—I, IV, V. By exploring, children will discover other chords they can use in harmonization.

Children's harmonizations and second parts may not always conform to the adult perception of what sounds "good." As little should be made of this as possible. Music history abounds with examples of music considered discordant by one generation being accepted by the next.

USING THE EXPRESSIVE ELEMENTS IN CREATING

Tempo, dynamics, and timbre can add interest to the simplest improvisations and compositions of children. Returning to the second-grade rhythm composition given earlier (Example 30), ask the children to decide on a tempo and to indicate that tempo with the correct word. Ask them to show at what dynamic level they wish their composition to be performed and to insert crescendos or decrescendos. They can decide which rhythm instruments should perform the *a* phrases and which instruments with contrasting timbre should perform the *b* section. In other words, they can make musical decisions that will enhance their compositions and make them more interesting.

EXAMPLE 30

The same sort of choices should be made with respect to their invented texts and melodies, while in the area of harmony, their decisions as to which melody instrument sounds best playing which parts demand a real understanding of the timbral qualities of the instruments.

CONCLUSION

Creating with music is no more difficult than creating with words. Each involves using the vocabulary one knows in different ways to invent something that is one's own. That "vocabulary" in music is made up of text, rhythm melody, harmony, tempo, timbre, and dynamics. By exploring each of these in turn and by experimenting with each, children may acquire the skills and the knowledge they need to create music.

ACTIVITIES

1. Pick a song. Create new words for it to celebrate a holiday.
2. Take a familiar nursery rhyme. Set it to a new meter and rhythm. Compose a tune for it in *aaba* form, using only five notes—C, D, E, F, G. Indicate tempo and dynamic levels.
3. Plan a creative activity for use with a third-grade class. Describe exactly what preparatory steps you will take and how you will conduct the activity.

II

THE SUBJECT IS MUSIC

The activities through which children experience music—singing, moving, playing, reading, writing, listening, and creating—have been explored in the first section of this book. These activities possess value as a part of any curriculum in music. Children who engage in them will probably enjoy their music classes.

However, there is more to the teaching of music than simply leading children through a series of musical experiences, enjoyable as they may be. Music is a subject, a discipline, like any other, with a body of knowledge and related skills. As a result of the musical experiences, children should arrive at certain important understandings: They should be led to infer *concepts* about music and to develop *skills* in music. This can happen only if the teacher has a clear perception of what that knowledge is and what those related skills are, and can order children's experiences so that they result in systematic and sequential concept inference and skill development.

To do this most effectively, it is necessary to examine the separate parts, the building blocks, that make up the totality we call music. These are generally referred to as the elements of music: rhythm, melody, harmony, form, tempo, timbre, and dynamics.

The next chapters will focus on these elements and on the most important understandings necessary in each for the implementation of any comprehensive curriculum of music education.

CHAPTER 9

BEAT, METER, AND RHYTHM
The Movement of Music

BEAT AND METER

What Is Beat?

UNDERLYING MOST MUSIC, THERE IS A REGULAR, RECURRING STRESS GENERALLY REFERRED TO AS "THE BEAT." For example:

Yan - kee   Doo - dle   went   to   town   a -
♥   ♥   ♥   ♥

Rid - ing   on   a   po   -   ny.
♥   ♥   ♥   ♥

Stuck   a   fea - ther   in   his   hat   and
♥   ♥   ♥   ♥

Called   it   mac - a - ro   -   ni
♥   ♥   ♥   ♥

The beat is steady, like the ticking of a large clock:

Yan-kee   Doo-dle Keep it   up
Yan-kee   Doo-dle Dan-   dy
Mind the Mu-sic   And the   steps and
With the Girls be han-   dy!

Perform Example 1 and the rhyme "Jack and Jill." Tap the beats on your lap.

EXAMPLE 1 "Old MacDonald"

In some music, the beat is heavy and obvious. Most children's singing games and dances have very pronounced beat. Most popular music, and particularly "rock," has an easily identifiable beat.

In other music, the beat may be lighter or even barely perceptible. In some of the music of Debussy and some twentieth-century works by composers such as John Cage and R. Murray Schafer, it is not easy to aurally perceive a beat. But the beat is there in most music. It is one of the principal unifying forces in music.

What Is Meter?

BEATS MOVE IN REGULAR GROUPS, DEFINED BY STRESSED OR ACCENTED BEATS. For example:

In "Yankee Doodle," the beats are moving in groups of twos, with the first beat more accented than the second.

Sing "Yankee Doodle" (Example 2). Slap your lap with a pronounced sound on the accented beats. When music is moving in twos, as in "Yankee Doodle," it is called *duple meter.* There is a number at the beginning of the song to indicate this.

EXAMPLE 2

We can conduct music that moves in twos by placing the right hand just below eye level and bringing the hand and arm down to about waist level on the accented beat allowing it to bounce back up to its original place on the second or unaccented beat. The arm should be away from the body, relaxed and free, never stiff.

The two beats we are conducting are called the downbeat (the accented beat):

and the upbeat (the unaccented beat):

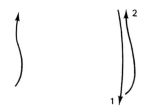

Sing "Yankee Doodle," "Twinkle, Twinkle, Little Star," and "Old Mac-Donald." Conduct them as you sing.

The three songs you just sang all move in twos. Music does not always move in twos. For example:

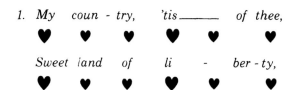

2. *La - ven - der's   blue,   dil - ly   dil - ly,*

♥   ♥   ♥   ♥   ♥   ♥

La - ven - der's   green_____.

♥   ♥   ♥   ♥   ♥   ♥

When   I   am   King,   dil - ly   dil - ly,

♥   ♥   ♥   ♥   ♥   ♥

You   shall   be   Queen_____.

♥   ♥   ♥   ♥   ♥   ♥

3. *Si   -   lent   night!_____*

♥   ♥   ♥   ♥   ♥   ♥

Ho   -   ly   night!_____

♥   ♥   ♥   ♥   ♥   ♥

These songs move in threes, or *simple triple meter.* In printed music, the number 3 is given at the beginning of the song (see Example 3).

EXAMPLE 3

| | My | coun - | try, | 'tis | of | thee, |
| | God | save | our | gra - | cious | Queen, |

To conduct music moving in threes, we must add a motion between the downbeat and the upbeat. The arm must move sideways to the right, away from the body, for the second beat:

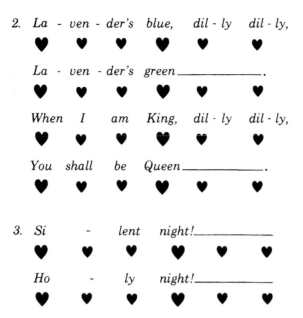

Conduct triple meter as you sing "My Country, 'Tis of Thee," "Lavender's Blue," and "Silent Night."

Sometimes, music moves in fours, or *simple quadruple meter.*

Glo - ry, glo·ry, hal·le·lu   -   ia!_____

♥   ♥   ♥   ♥   ♥   ♥   ♥   ♥

Glo - ry, glo·ry, hal·le·lu   -   ia!_____

♥   ♥   ♥   ♥   ♥   ♥   ♥   ♥

Glo - ry, glo·ry, hal·le·lu   -   ia!   His

♥   ♥   ♥   ♥   ♥   ♥   ♥   ♥

Truth   is   march-ing   on._____

♥   ♥   ♥   ♥   ♥   ♥   ♥   ♥

Many hymns and marches are in simple quadruple meter (Example 4).

EXAMPLE 4

Joy   to   the world!   the   Lord   is   come;

To conduct quadruple meter, we must add a new motion; the arm must move toward the left on beat two:

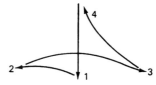

Conduct quadruple meter while singing "The Battle Hymn of the Republic" and "Joy to the World."

ALL METERS MOVE IN TWOS, THREES, OR FOURS OR IN COMBINATIONS THEREOF.

Barlines and Measures

In the earliest days of written notation in the Western world, there was nothing to indicate where accents should occur in music. The notation of Gregorian chants sung by monks in their worship simply indicated the higher and lower movement of pitches, while the placement of the text implied whatever stresses were to occur. As time went on, a need was felt to regularize the accenting or stressing at specific points in the music. Barlines were placed before accented beats:

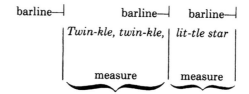

The barline tells us that the next beat must be accented.

The space between barlines is referred to as a *measure*. At the end of a piece, there is a *double bar* to show that there is no more.

If we count beats from one barline to the next, or from one accented beat to the next, we know how many beats are in a measure—whether the music is moving in twos, threes, or fours. This tells us what number must be shown on the top half of the staff at the beginning of the music, a 2, a 3, or a 4.

Where should the barlines go in the following songs? Before which words? Is the song in duple, triple, or quadruple meter?

1. *This old   man,   He played one*
   He played knick-knack On my   thumb.

2. *Oh where, oh where has my Lit-tle dog gone_____*

3. *Are you sleep-ing, Are you sleep-ing,*

The "beat" shown in all the examples given thus far as ♥ is equal to the quarter note: ♩.

The quarter-note value is shown in meter signs as the number 4. Meter signs show both how many beats are in a measure (2, 3, or 4) and the kind of note we are counting as equal to one beat:

2 (how many)   3 (how many)   4 (how many)
4 (what kind)   4 (what kind)   4 (what kind)

Upbeat

All the songs we have sung so far have begun on the downbeat, the accented beat. Sing "Happy Birthday."

3/4 *Hap-py birth - day   to   you,___*
Hap-py birth - day   to   you,___
Hap-py birth - day,   dear   Su - san,
Hap-py birth - day   to   you.___

How is "Happy Birthday" moving? In threes. On which of the beats does "Happy Birthday" begin? The third, the beat we conduct as an upbeat. Many songs begin on the upbeat rather than on the downbeat. Where are the two missing beats? Sing the song through again to find them. They are at the end of the song.

Simple Meters

Pulses: Subdivisions of the Beat

IF ONE THINKS OF MUSIC AS A SORT OF ARCHITECTURE, THE FOUNDATION IS THE ACCENTED OR METRIC BEAT, THE FIRST FLOOR IS THE REGULAR BEAT, AND THE SECOND FLOOR IS THE PULSE, THE REGULAR SUBDIVISIONS OF THAT BEAT:

Where the beat is the quarter note, ♩, the pulses move in eighth notes, ♪. In all simple meters, there is a 2-to-1 relationship between pulse and beat (see Example 5).

EXAMPLE 5

IN ALL SIMPLE METERS, THE EVEN SUBDIVISIONS OF THE BEAT—THE PULSES—MOVE IN TWOS.

Clap the pulses and step the beats or tap them with one foot while singing Examples 6–8.

EXAMPLE 6 "This Old Man" (²⁄₄)

This old man, he played one, he played knick-knack on my thumb.

Knick-knack pad-dy-whack, give a dog a bone, This old man went rol-ling home.

EXAMPLE 7 "Lavender's Blue" (³⁄₄)

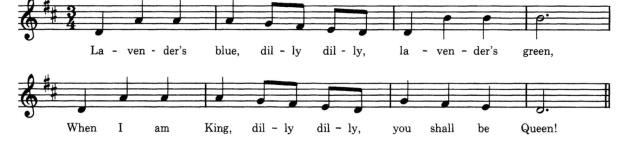

La - ven - der's blue, dil - ly dil - ly, la - ven - der's green,

When I am King, dil - ly dil - ly, you shall be Queen!

EXAMPLE 8 "Brother John" (⁴⁄₄)

Are you sleep - ing, Are you sleep - ing, Broth - er John,

Broth - er John? Morn - ing bells are ring - ing,

morn - ing bells are ring - ing, ding, dang, dong! ding, dang, dong!

Compound Meters

While all meters move in twos, threes, or fours, or in combinations thereof, not all meters are simple. Say the following nursery rhyme. Tap the accented and unaccented beats. How is it moving?

Hickory dickory dock,
The mouse ran up the clock,
The clock struck one, the mouse ran down,
Hickory dickory dock.

It is moving in twos. It is in duple meter. We would conduct it as we conducted "Yankee Doodle."

Say the rhyme and conduct it.

There are two felt beats in each measure. There is one accented beat in each measure.

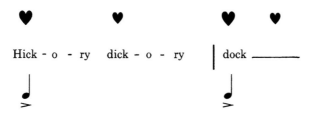

In spite of the sameness of the conducting pattern, the accented beats, and the beats, "Hickory Dickory Dock" does not feel the same as "Twinkle, Twinkle, Little Star." The difference lies in the movement of pulses over the beat, in the regular subdivisions of the beat.

In "Twinkle, Twinkle," the pulses, or eighth notes (♪), moved in groups of twos (♫).

Tap the subdivisions of the beat this time as you sing "Row Your Boat":

Row, row, row your boat,
Gently down the stream,
Merrily, merrily, merrily, merrily,
Life is but a dream.

How are the pulses moving? In groups of threes: ♫♩.

IN COMPOUND METER, THE PULSES—THE REGULAR SUBDIVISIONS OF THE BEAT—ARE FELT IN THREES (Example 9).

EXAMPLE 9

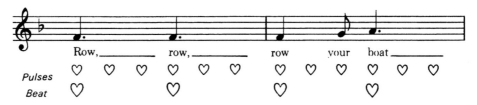

The meter sign in compound meters does not tell us about conducting beats as it does in simple meters; instead, it tells us about the pulses, the subdivisions of the beat. How many pulses are in a measure in "Row Your Boat"? Six. The top number of the meter sign must be a 6.

What kind of note is the pulse? An eighth note, ♪. The bottom number of the meter sign must be an 8. Therefore, the meter sign for "Row Your Boat" is ⁶₈ or ⁶⁄₈.

As with simple meters, compound meters may be duple (conducted in twos—Example 10); triple (conducted in threes—Example 11); or even quadruple (conducted in fours—Example 12).

EXAMPLE 10

EXAMPLE 11

EXAMPLE 12

Compound triple and quadruple do not occur often in songs.

How Can We Tell the Meter of a Piece by Listening or Singing?

When listening to or singing a piece:

1. Tap the beats.
2. Listen for the stressed or accented beats. How is the music moving? In twos, threes, or fours?
3. Conduct the music to check your answer.
4. Now, clap the subdivisions of the beat. Are they moving in twos (♪♪—simple meter) or in threes (♪♪♪—compound meter)?

Your answer will usually be simple duple, triple, or quadruple, or compound duple.

How can we tell by looking at music what the meter is, what the conducting beat should be?

Look on the staff, near the beginning of the first line of music. Before any notes occur, there are two numbers on the staff, one over the other. They look somewhat like a fraction, but they are not, and they should not be thought of as such. Notice that there is no line between them.

The bottom number tells what kind of note is being counted. It is most commonly a 4, representing the quarter note, or an 8, representing the eighth note.

The top number tells how many quarter notes or eighth notes could occur in a measure. In simple meters, it will be 2 or 3 or 4. In compound meters, it will usually be 6 or very occasionally 9 or 12. Sometimes, instead of a number, you may see **C**. This is called *common time* and is simply another way of indicating $\frac{4}{4}$.[1]

All these meters, simple and compound, may be conducted as moving in twos ($\frac{2}{4}$, $\frac{6}{8}$), threes ($\frac{3}{4}$, $\frac{9}{8}$), or fours ($\frac{4}{4}$, $\frac{12}{8}$).

"Cut Time"

The bottom number of the meter sign is not always a 4 for the quarter note, ♩, or an 8 for the eighth note, ♪. It can be a 2 for the half note, ♩. The top number still tells us how many beats to conduct and is most frequently 2.

This meter, usually performed in a faster tempo, is known as *cut time* and may also be shown as the **C** of common time with a slash through it, **¢**. Many marches, singing games, and folk dances are in cut time. We feel two beats to the measure, even though in counting we will find the equivalent of four quarter notes in each measure. The beat note is ♩ rather than ♩ (see Example 13). The musical term for $\frac{2}{2}$, cut time, is *alla breve*, Italian words that mean "in a short manner."

EXAMPLE 13

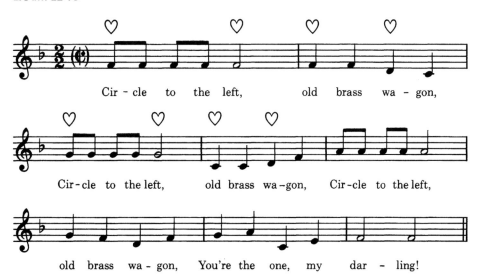

Cir - cle to the left, old brass wa - gon,

Cir-cle to the left, old brass wa –gon, Cir-cle to the left,

old brass wa - gon, You're the one, my dar – ling!

Asymmetric Meters

Asymmetric meters combine movement in twos and threes in each measure. Keeping a steady quarter-note beat, read Example 14 aloud. Call the quarter notes *ta*'s. Now accent every other quarter note (Example 15). When we do this, we have created a "duple" meter.

---

[1]*Common time:* Four quarter notes to the bar, written $\frac{4}{4}$ or **C**. The latter sign does not stand for "common" but derives from an obsolete way of indicating time values; it dates from the period when triple time (called "perfect") was indicated by a full circle and quadruple time (called "imperfect") by a broken circle.

EXAMPLE 14

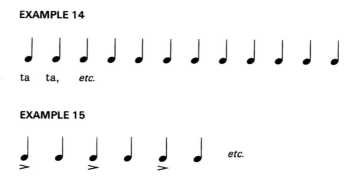

ta   ta,   *etc.*

EXAMPLE 15

Next, read the exercise with accents on the first of each three quarter notes (Example 16). Here we have a clear example of a triple meter.

EXAMPLE 16

Now, let us combine these two ideas. Perform 2 + 3 + 2 + 3 + 2 (Example 17). The feeling we get of being off-balance is characteristic of asymmetric meters. Threes and twos may be arranged in any combination, as in Example 18. Either quarter notes or eighth notes may be the beat.

EXAMPLE 17

EXAMPLE 18

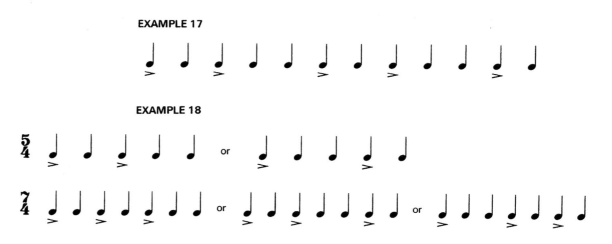

Sing "Brother John" in ⅜. As you sing, slap laps on accented beats and clap hands on unaccented ones. Your clapping pattern will be:

Slap clap clap slap clap slap clap
 >   -   -   >   -   >   -

Summary

All metric music moves in twos or threes or in combinations or multiples of twos and threes. We can identify the meter of a heard piece by tapping its beat, locating the accented beats, and counting beats from one accent to the next. Next, by tapping pulses and discovering whether they are moving in groups of twos or threes, or combinations of twos and threes, we can determine whether the meter is simple (♪♩), compound (♩♩♩), or asymmetric (♩♩ ♩♩♩).

The numbers at the beginning of printed music tell us what to conduct in simple meters:

2 for $\frac{2}{4}$, $\frac{2}{2}$
3 for $\frac{3}{4}$, $\frac{3}{2}$
4 for $\frac{4}{4}$

For most compound meter songs, we conduct the beats rather than the pulses:

2 for $\frac{6}{8}$, $\frac{6}{4}$
3 for $\frac{9}{8}$
4 for $\frac{12}{8}$

ACTIVITIES

1. When listening to the radio, tapes, or records, tap the beat. Listen for the accented beats. Is the music moving in twos, threes, or fours? Conduct it.

2. Using twelve quarter notes as your basic beats, place accents to create
   Duple meter
   Triple meter
   Quadruple meter
   Asymmetric meter
Perform each pattern you have notated.

3. The children's rhyme "Baa, Baa, Black Sheep" is in simple duple meter.
   Baa, baa, black sheep, have you any wool?
   Yes sir, yes sir, three bags full;
   One for my Master, one for my Dame,
   One for the little boy who lives down the lane.
Perform it in:
   Simple triple meter
   Compound duple meter
   Asymmetric meter

RHYTHM

Over all the ingredients discussed thus far—over the accented beats, the beats, and the pulses—moves the rhythm of music. Metric accent, beat, and pulse may be the same in many songs; however, the rhythm is unique to each song.

RHYTHM IS MADE UP OF PATTERNS OF LONGER AND SHORTER SOUNDS AND SILENCES OVER THE BEAT. IN SONGS, IT IS THE WAY THE WORDS GO.

Quarter Notes and Eighth Notes in Rhythm

SOUNDS AND SILENCES MAY BE EVENLY ARRANGED OVER BEATS.

The rhythm of a song may in some phrases contain one sound on one beat, as in Example 19. When this happens, the singing and the conducting beats coincide, with one word or syllable equal in length to one conducting gesture.

EXAMPLE 19

Are   you   sleep - ing

♡   ♡   ♡   ♡

At other times, the rhythm may contain two even sounds over each beat, as in Example 20.

EXAMPLE 20

Yan-kee Doo –dle went to town a-

♡   ♡   ♡   ♡

Often, in the rhythm, there is a combination of beats with one sound and beats with two sounds, as in Example 21.

EXAMPLE 21

Called it   mac - a - ro   –   ni.

♡   ♡   ♡   ♡

Quarter notes (♩, *ta*) may move at about a comfortable walking pace. Eighth notes (♪, *ti*) must be precisely twice as fast as the quarter note—in a strict, even, 2-to-1 ratio. Tap or tap and say the patterns in Example 22; be sure to establish your walking beat first.

EXAMPLE 22

Paired eighth notes are an even subdivision into twos over the beat. Other even subdivisions are also possible:

Into fours: sixteenth notes ♬♬

Into threes in compound meter: ♪♪♪ or as triplets ♪♪♪

Rest

Sometimes, there is a place in the music where the beat goes on but the tune does not. There is a silence. In music this is called a *rest*. A rest of one beat's duration in $\frac{2}{4}$, $\frac{3}{4}$, or $\frac{4}{4}$ looks like this: and is called a *quarter rest*. It is equal in duration to a quarter note. It indicates a full beat of silence. Tap the beat on your desk, lightly with fingertips. Say the patterns in Example 23 using *ta*'s, *ti*'s and *ti-ka*'s. Be careful not to voice anything on the rests but to continue tapping the beat.

EXAMPLE 23

The following activities give practice in performing even arrangements of sounds over beats.

1. Sing the rhythm to this verse of "Yankee Doodle" in *ti*'s and *ta*'s while tapping the beat with fingertips on the desk.

    Yankee Doodle went to town a-
    Riding on a pony.
    Stuck a feather in his cap and
    Called it macaroni.

2. Say the rhyme "Pease Porridge Hot" with words. Then say it again with *ti*'s and *ta*'s while maintaining the beat lightly on desks. Be careful to keep the beat going and not to speak on rests.

    Pease porridge hot,
    Pease porridge cold,
    Pease porridge in a pot
    Nine days old.

3. Create a rhythm composition sixteen beats long in $\frac{4}{4}$ meter, using eighth notes, quarter notes, and quarter rests. Give it to someone else in your class to read aloud. Was your notation clear enough and accurate enough to be performed by someone else?

4. In a school music text series, find ten examples of songs in simple meter with no rhythmic figures other than quarter notes, eighth notes in pairs, and quarter rests. Find three examples with a four-sixteenth-note grouping. Be ready to perform the rhythm of one of these for the class.

The Half Note and the Whole Note

SOMETIMES, NOTES ARE SOUNDED FOR MORE FULL BEATS THAN JUST ONE, as in Example 24.

A note that lasts for two beats in $\frac{2}{4}$, $\frac{3}{4}$, and $\frac{4}{4}$ is called a *half note,* ♩ (*too*). It is important to continue the sound of the half note right up to the beginning of the next note. It must sound through the full second beat and stop only at the beginning of the third beat. Think of the half note as two quarter notes tied together (Example 25). It must be held for the duration of two quarter notes or two full beats.

EXAMPLE 24

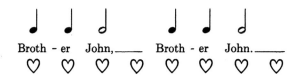

Broth - er   John, ____   Broth - er   John. ____

EXAMPLE 25

Sing "Brother John" (Example 26) in *ta*'s, *ti*'s, and *too*'s.

EXAMPLE 26

Are   you   sleep - ing,   Are   you   sleep - ing,   Broth - er   John,

Broth - er   John?   Morn - ing   bells   are   ring - ing,

Morn-ing bells are ring - ing,   Ding,   dang,   dong,   Ding,   dang,   ding.

A whole note in $\frac{4}{4}$ is equal to four full beats. Its sound does not stop until the beginning of the fifth beat (see Example 27).

EXAMPLE 27

Uneven Arrangements of Sounds over Beats

SOUNDS AND SILENCES MAY BE ARRANGED UNEVENLY OVER BEATS.

Sometimes, composers wish to emphasize a particular word in a text or a particular note in a melody. One way of doing that is by making that note a bit longer, and consequently making the one following it a bit shorter.

The rhythm in Example 28 is admittedly dull. (Read it aloud.)

EXAMPLE 28

By simply lengthening some notes and making the ones that follow them shorter, we create a more interesting rhythm —one that underlines the meaning of the text (Example 29).

EXAMPLE 29

My coun - try 'tis of thee, Sweet land of
God save our grac - ious Queen, Long live our

li - ber - ty, Of thee I sing._____
no - ble Queen, God save the Queen._____

The rhythm has been altered in only two places from the first example, but the result is far more interesting musically.

The "value" of the dot after a note is always half the value of the note itself. However, that mathematical knowledge is not much help with accurate rhythmic performance. More to the point, think of the pattern whenever you see a dotted quarter note.

1. Say and tap:

ta   ti ti

2. Now tie ♩ to ♪ and add the letter *m* where the first *ti* occurs:

tam - ti

The dot after the quarter note is equal to an eighth note.

If we tap eighth-note pulses, the dotted quarter note is equal to three eighths:

♩.   ♪
♪ ♪ ♪ ♪

Practice saying the rhythms in Example 30 with *ta*'s, *ti*'s, and *tam*'s.

EXAMPLE 30

Another common uneven rhythmic arrangement is simple syncopation. Like dotted rhythms, syncopation is used to underline text and to create interest. Read Example 31. Now separate the eighth notes in the first two measures. Put one before and one after the quarter note. Remember to make the quarter note last as long as two eighth notes. The rhythm is now as shown in Example 32.

EXAMPLE 31

EXAMPLE 32

The longer sound beginning after the first beat and before the second gives a feeling of importance to that note (Example 33).

EXAMPLE 33

Do Lord,   oh,   do Lord,   oh,   do re - mem - ber   me!

ACTIVITIES

1. Practice saying the pattern of syncopation in Example 34. It may help to tap the eighth-note pulse as you say the *ti*'s and *ta*'s.

2. In a music series text, find examples of the syncopation pattern in ⅔ or ¼ meter.

3. Create and notate a rhythm composition eight measures long in meter. Use syncopation in it.

EXAMPLE 34

Other Rhythmic Figures

Most other rhythmic figures are best learned by comparing them to ones already known:

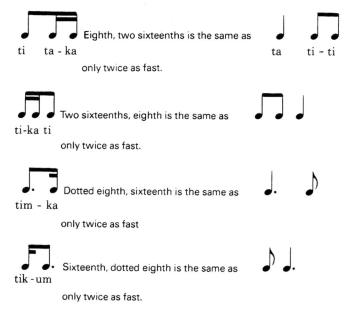

Eighth, two sixteenths is the same as only twice as fast.

ti ta - ka ta ti - ti

Two sixteenths, eighth is the same as only twice as fast.

ti-ka ti

Dotted eighth, sixteenth is the same as only twice as fast

tim - ka

Sixteenth, dotted eighth is the same as only twice as fast.

tik - um

EXAMPLE 35

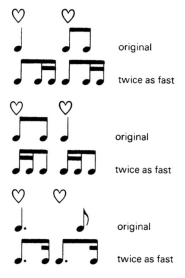

original

twice as fast

original

twice as fast

original

twice as fast

If we relate these shorter rhythmic figures to the eighth-note pulse, it becomes obvious where the sounds occur (Example 36).

EXAMPLE 36

ti   ti - ka   ti - ka - ti   tim -   ka   tik - um

Rhythms in Compound Meters

One other set of rhythmic figures should be discussed—those encountered in § and other compound meters. While the mathematical note values are the same in § as in ²⁄₄, ³⁄₄, or ⁴⁄₄, the inner relationship among notes is different. Note groupings in § are in threes over the conducting beat. Rhythm patterns within § are equal to three eighth notes (see Example 37).

EXAMPLE 37

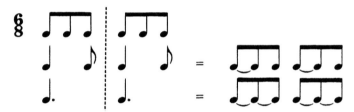

§ is an extremely symmetrical meter. Each half of the measure usually contains the equivalent of three eighth notes. Only rarely in § is a note value carried through the middle of the measure.

Practice the § patterns in Example 38. Say them with *ti*'s, *ta*'s, and *tam*'s while tapping the duple conducting beat.

EXAMPLE 38

If the text requires more sounds than the three-eighth-note grouping allows, one or more of the three is changed into two sixteenth notes (Example 39). However, the feeling of grouping into threes over the conducting beat is rarely altered rhythmically in §.

EXAMPLE 39

ti - ti - ka - ti

Sometimes, there are dotted rhythms in ⁶⁄₈. As in ²⁄₄, ³⁄₄, and ⁴⁄₄, the dot simply lengthens the note it follows (Example 40).

EXAMPLE 40

tim - ka ti

ACTIVITIES

1. Find ten examples of songs in ⁶⁄₈ meter. Choose one to read aloud using *ti*'s, *ta*'s, and *tam*'s, and any other necessary syllables.

2. Create and notate a rhythm four measures long in ⁶⁄₈ meter.

CONCLUSION

Beat is the most fundamental aspect of music. Nearly all music has a regular recurring stress, known as beat. Some beats are accented, or heavier than others. To determine meter, we count from one accented beat to the next. All music moves in twos or threes, or in multiples and combinations of twos and threes.

The beat may be subdivided evenly into "little beats," or pulses. In simple meters, there are two pulses over each conducting beat. In compound meters, there are three pulses over each conducting beat.

Rhythm is the grouping into patterns of longer and shorter sounds and silences over the beat; it is, in songs, "the way the words go." In the rhythm of a piece of music, there may be one sound on one beat or two or more sounds on one beat. The sounds may be evenly or unevenly arranged over beats. Some sounds may last two or three or four full beats, or occasionally even longer. In songs, the rhythm usually underlines some aspect of the text. It is related to the way we might say the words, but it is more measured and precise.

Beat and meter give unity to music. Rhythm supplies variety.

CHAPTER 10

MELODY
The Shape of Music

The Farmer in the Dell,
The Farmer in the Dell,
Heigh Ho, the Derry-O,
The Farmer in the Dell!

Three blind mice,
Three blind mice,
See how they run!
See how they run!
They all ran after the farmer's wife;
She cut off their tails with a carving knife!
Did you see such a sight in your life as
Three blind mice!

MELODIC MOVEMENT AND CONTOUR

For most English-speaking people, merely reading the familiar words of the preceding rhymes will cause a melody to pop into their heads. It may be twenty years, or fifty years, since they have sung or heard either of these old songs, but the tune will still be there, stored, to be called into consciousness by the words.

A melody, once firmly acquired, is never completely lost. Even when we can't bring the whole to mind, we can generally reproduce characteristic fragments of the original. It is melody, more than any other element of music, that conveys to us the emotional content of that music.

The word *melody* refers to the general contour of a piece of music, the particular and unique combination of sounds—some higher, some lower, some repeated—that makes each piece different from others.

Essentially, MELODIES MAY MOVE IN ONLY SIX WAYS:

1. THEY MAY GO HIGHER.
2. THEY MAY GO LOWER.
3. THEY MAY HAVE REPEATED NOTES.

Further,

4. THEY MAY GO HIGHER OR LOWER BY SMALL *STEPS*.
5. THEY MAY DO SO BY SKIPPING ONE PITCH IN BETWEEN *(SKIPS)*.
6. THEY MAY DO SO BY *LEAPS* OVER TWO OR MORE NOTES.

MELODIES GENERALLY HAVE SOME PARTS THAT ARE THE SAME, TO GIVE THEM UNITY:

Are you sleeping?
Are you sleeping?

AND SOME PARTS THAT ARE DIFFERENT, TO GIVE THEM VARIETY:

Morning bells are ringing,
Ding, dang, dong_____

MELODIES HAVE BREATHING PLACES (PHRASE ENDINGS). THEY TEND TO HAVE A FEELING OF INCOMPLETENESS AT POINTS IN THE MIDDLE:

London bridge is falling down . . .

AND OF COMPLETENESS AT THE END:

My fair lady!

MELODIES USUALLY END ON THE *TONAL CENTER* OR *KEYNOTE* (*do* OR 1 OF THE SCALE).

Melodies of songs generally emphasize the song text. They follow the flow of the words, and if they are *good* songs, dramatic points in the text also are dramatic points in the melody. Look at Example 1. In this example, the melody is at its highest point where the farmer's wife is alerting her husband to the fact that a fox is among the geese.

EXAMPLE 1

"John,   John,   the   gray   goose   is   gone!"

EACH MELODY HAS A *SHAPE* OR *CONTOUR*. Look at Example 2 ("Brother John"). The overall contour is one of an ascending melodic line for the first half and a descending melodic line for the second half (Example 3). Most of the "Brother John" melody is stepwise, with only occasional skips. At the end of the song, there are *leaps* when we sing "Ding, dang, dong."

EXAMPLE 2

EXAMPLE 3

In "Joy to the World," again the movement is largely *stepwise,* but this song begins with a descending melody. Its contour is essentially from high to low. There is a *leap* on "heaven" in the last phrase (Example 4). Example 5 shows the contour of "Joy to the World."

EXAMPLE 4

Joy   to   the world!   the   Lord   is   come;   And   hea - ven

EXAMPLE 5

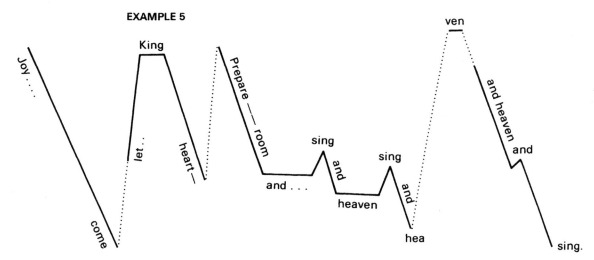

Contours give the general shape of a melody, but they do not show accurately the size of the steps, skips, and leaps. For that, notation is needed, and at least *one* staff line. Let us use the G line of the musical staff. Example 6 shows where it sounds on the piano (that is, to the right of the first black key in the group of three).

EXAMPLE 6

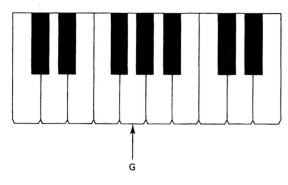

We will use a G-clef sign at the beginning of the music. The word *clef* simply means "key" (such as a house key). In music, the *clef sign* curls around a particular line or space to identify it for us. This clef, the G clef, curling around the G line, tells us the name and the pitch of notes on that line (Example 7).

EXAMPLE 7

What kind of melodic movement does the line in Example 7 have? Only one—repeated notes.

Sing the line. You may call the notes G, 1, or *do.*

A melody of nothing but repeated notes is certainly dull. Vary it by singing every *other* note one step higher, on A. (Example 8 shows the location of A on the piano.) Sing this melody. Call the note above G A or *re* (Example 9).

EXAMPLE 8

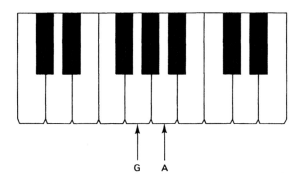

EXAMPLE 9

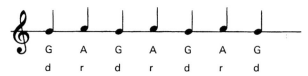

The melody becomes a bit more interesting with two notes instead of one. By adding some rhythmic variations, we can make it still more interesting; sing it in the rhythm indicated in Example 10.

EXAMPLE 10

We have tried a melody moving *higher* by step; let us try one moving *lower*. Call the note *below* the line *do.* Its absolute name is F. (*Any* note may be the keynote, *do* or 1.) See Examples 11 and 12.

EXAMPLE 11

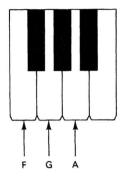

EXAMPLE 12

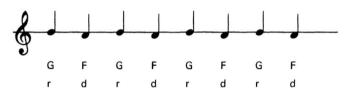

Now let's use all three notes (F = *do* or 1). See Example 13. The melody has steps ascending, steps descending, and repeated notes. Read Example 14. It has the same melodic elements; sing it with A, G, F, and with *m-r-d*. Then play it and sing it with words.

EXAMPLE 13

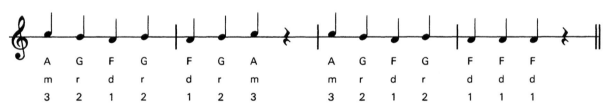

EXAMPLE 14

This song may be moved to a different place on the staff—a higher place beginning on B—but the *melody* remains the same. Sing and play Example 15. Now try it in a lower place—beginning on E above middle C (see Examples 16 and 17). There is no staff line for middle C, so we must make a small line—a *ledger line*—through that note so that it is clear that it *is* the next step below D. When music moves by step, the notes always move from line to adjoining space or from space to adjoining line.

EXAMPLE 15

EXAMPLE 16

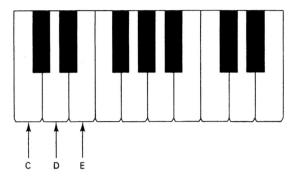

EXAMPLE 17

ACTIVITIES

1. Draw the contour of a melody you think others in your class may know well, such as "Twinkle, Twinkle, Little Star," "Here We Go 'round the Mulberry Bush," or "The Farmer in the Dell." Show your contour to the class. Give the class a choice of three or four song titles. Can they identify your song correctly from the contour you have drawn?

2. Compose a four-measure melody in ²⁄₄ meter on the notes A, G, and F (F = *do*). Your melody should *end* on F. Use ♩, ♫ and 𝄽 in the rhythm. Be ready to sing or play your composition to the class.

THE MUSICAL STAFF

So far, we have used only part of the musical staff. We needed only two lines for "Hot Cross Buns." The full staff has five lines (Example 18).

EXAMPLE 18

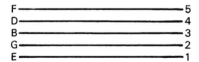

Lines

We count staff lines from the *bottom* up. The first line (E pitch) is the one on the bottom. The fifth line (high F) is the one on the top. AS NOTES MOVE ON THE STAFF FROM THE FIRST LINE TO THE FIFTH, PITCH IS INCREASINGLY HIGHER. AS NOTES MOVE FROM THE FIFTH LINE TOWARD THE FIRST, THE PITCHES BECOME INCREASINGLY LOWER. A note to be "on a line" must have the line running through it (Example 19).

EXAMPLE 19

Spaces

In between the lines, there are four spaces. These also are counted from the bottom up (Example 20). Notes in spaces sit between the lines (Example 21).

EXAMPLE 20

EXAMPLE 21

Example 22 shows the tune we sang using a two-line staff as it looks on a full staff in the key of G (G = *do*). Example 23 shows it in a higher place on the staff (E', D', C'). Its sound will be higher.

EXAMPLE 22

EXAMPLE 23

Notice that the note *stems* in Example 23 are pointing down. Note stems do not tell us anything about melody; they only indicate *duration*—the rhythm. So that they will fit well on the staff, we draw them *up* when the notehead is below the third line and *down* when the notehead is above the third line. *On* the third line the stem may go either way.

Scales

In the preceding pages, we have read and sung two- and three-note melodies, using every note from the ledger line below the staff to the fourth space on the staff.[1]

IF WE ARRANGE ALL THESE NOTES IN ORDER FROM THE LOWEST TO THE HIGHEST, WE HAVE A MAJOR SCALE. Sing and play Example 24. The scale is a melody everyone knows. Looking at the staff, we see that all the steps in the scale appear to be the same size—line, space, line, space, and so on—for eight notes. However, if we look at the keyboard, it quickly becomes obvious that the "steps" are not all the same size (Example 25). Between C and D, there is a black note, a half step called C-*sharp* (♯) or D-*flat* (♭). Between D and E, there is a black note, a half step called D-*sharp* (♯) or

---

[1]The musical "alphabet" goes from A to G and then begins again.

E-*flat* (♭). However, there is *no* black note between E and F; E to F is *not* a whole step—it is a *half* step; it is the same size as from C to C-sharp or from E to E-flat.

EXAMPLE 24

EXAMPLE 25

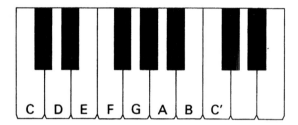

Where is another half step on the keyboard? B to C is a half step, too.

Play C to D; this is the sound of a whole step. Now play C to C-sharp; this is the sound of a half step. Play E to F; this is the sound of a half step. Play B to C; this is the sound of a half step.

THE MELODY WE KNOW AS A MAJOR SCALE HAS BOTH WHOLE STEPS AND HALF STEPS. To understand key signatures, we must know the pattern of those whole steps and half steps. It is

```
C
B >  half step   < 8
                   7
    whole step
A                  6
    whole step
G                  5
    whole step
F
E >  half step   < 4
                   3
    whole step
D                  2
    whole step
C                  1
```

Note that 3 to 4 and 7 to 8 are *smaller intervals*; they are always *half steps* in the major scale.

KEY SIGNATURES

Flats

No matter on what key or what note we begin a major scale, the preceding pattern of whole steps and half steps must be observed. Let us try a scale on F:

```
F  8
E  7
D  6
  C  5
  B
      4
A  3
G  2
F  1
```

If we play only white keys, it is quickly apparent that one note, B, sounds wrong—it is too high. The half step needed between pitches 3 and 4 isn't there; it is between 4 and 5 instead. To correct the sound, we must substitute the note that is a half step lower: B-flat. The tune of the scale is now "right," and its whole-step–half-step pattern is now correct.

In printed music, the need for B-flat in the key of F is indicated immediately after the G clef (Example 26). It tells us that we are in the key of F *major*.

EXAMPLE 26

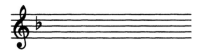

Let us carry this major-scale pattern to another place on the keyboard. Let us begin on a "black note"—B-flat:

```
B♭  8
A   7
G   6
  F   5
  E
        4
D   3
C   2
B♭  1
```

EXAMPLE 27

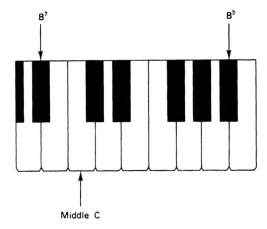

Middle C

Because we began and ended with B-flat, the half step from 7 to 8 (A to B♭) is in place. Where is there a problem? From D to E is a whole step, but from 3 to 4 must be a half step. A lower sound is needed—E-flat rather than E.

In the key of B-flat, the key signature shows *two* flats—B-flat and E-flat (Example 28).

EXAMPLE 28

As we apply the scale pattern to various starting pitches, we can discover the need for three flats, four flats, even six flats, to create the major-scale melody beginning on different keys.

AN EASY WAY TO FIND THE KEYNOTE (*do* OR THE FIRST DEGREE OF THE SCALE) TO KNOW "WHAT KEY YOU ARE IN" IS TO CALL THE *LAST* FLAT—THE ONE FARTHEST TO THE RIGHT IN THE KEY SIGNATURE—*fa* OR 4 AND SIMPLY COUNT OR SING BY STEPS DOWN THE LINES AND SPACES TO *do* OR 1. See Example 29.

EXAMPLE 29

Sharps

Sometimes, instead of a lower sound, we need a higher sound to make the correct major-scale tune:

```
        G   8
              7 >
      F
    < E   6
        D   5
        C   4
              3 >
        B
        A   2
        G   1
```

EXAMPLE 30

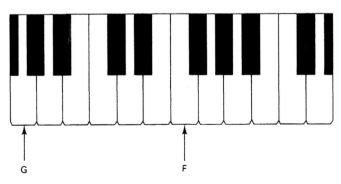

When we begin a scale on G and play only the white keys, it is apparent that the F is too low a sound; the half step occurs between 6 and 7 instead of between 7 and 8 as it must. To obtain a higher sound and the correct scale pattern, we must substitute F-sharp for F. The key signature for the key of G is *one sharp* (Example 31).

EXAMPLE 31   Key of G Major

Moving to the key of D, we find two places, F and C, where sharps are needed to produce the major-scale pattern:

```
D  8
    7>
 <C
  B  6

  A  5

  G  4
     3>
 <F
  E  2

  D  1
```

EXAMPLE 32   Key of D Major

As we apply the scale pattern to the keyboard, we find that we can start on *any* key and arrange a major scale with sharps simply by following the major-scale pattern.

As with flats, there is a quick way to "find" *do,* the keynote, by looking at the key signature. Call the last sharp to the right *ti* or 7. The note immediately above it is 8, *do,* the keynote. See Example 33.

EXAMPLE 33

Only C major needs no sharps or flats. Its natural scale pattern is the model for all other keys.

THE MINOR MODE AND MINOR SCALES

WHILE MOST ENGLISH-LANGUAGE SONGS AND MUCH OTHER MUSIC ARE IN MAJOR KEYS, SOME ARE IN *MINOR*. THE PATTERN OF MINOR SCALES IS DIFFERENT FROM THAT OF MAJOR SCALES, AND THE SOUND OF MUSIC IN THE MINOR MODES IS *VERY* DIFFERENT.

> *God rest you mer-ry, gen-tle-men,*
> *Let noth-ing you dis-may . . .*

If you begin on A on the piano and play eight white keys in ascending order, you have the *natural minor scale.*

What makes minor-mode music sound so different from major-mode music? Compare the two scales for the arrangement of whole steps and half steps:

```
MAJOR SCALE        NATURAL MINOR SCALE

 C  8  d>            A  8  l'
<B  7  t
                    G  7  s
 A  6  l
                    F  6  f>
 G  5  s           <E  5  m

 F  4  f>           D  4  r
<E  3  m
                    C  3  d>
 D  2  r           <B  2  t

 C  1  d            A  1  l
```

It is easy to see that the half steps are in different places. The *important* difference is in the *first three* notes of each scale. IN MAJOR SCALES, THESE ARE ALWAYS MADE OF TWO WHOLE STEPS; IN MINOR SCALES, THESE ARE ALWAYS ONE WHOLE STEP PLUS ONE HALF STEP. IT IS IN THE FIRST THREE DEGREES OF THE SCALE THAT THE "MAJORNESS" OR "MINORNESS" OF A MELODY IS ESTABLISHED.

The upper half of the minor-scale pattern also is different, but it exists in various patterns as the "natural minor," the "melodic minor," and the "harmonic minor." The *minor character* of all these minor scales is determined by the first three scale notes.

How can we tell whether a song or piece of music is in major or minor when we hear it?

For those with musically acute ears, the use of the lowered third scale degree in a melody is an immediate clue to the minor mode. However, minor-mode songs have a melodic quality so distinctive that even the youngest, most musically untrained children can distinguish and identify them. Many descriptive words have been used by children to describe minor: "dark," "sad," "melancholy," and, sometimes, "scary." Minor-mode music does not have to be any of those things. "God Rest You Merry, Gentlemen" is a cheerful and boisterous carol, yet it is in the minor mode.

To aurally distinguish major from minor, it is necessary only to listen to enough examples of each.

Identifying Minor-Mode Songs by Key Signature

To find the natural minor scale, we played from A to A' on the keyboard. No "black keys" were necessary.

Which major scale requires no black keys? C major.

A minor is related to C major. They have a common key signature: no sharps or flats. Every major key has its "related" minor key, and that related minor key is always the same distance below the major key as A is from C—one and one-half steps:

C
B   half step

       one step

A

Let us look at Example 34 and examine a few key signatures to determine where the minor scale would begin. You may observe that if the keynote in major is on a line, the keynote in minor is on the line below; if the keynote in major is in a space, the keynote in minor is in the space below.

EXAMPLE 34

| do | la | | do | la | | do | la | | do | la |
| F major | D minor | | B♭ major | G minor | | G major | E minor | | D major | B minor |

How can we tell whether a song is in a major or a minor key by looking at the music?

1. First we look at the key signature. Call the last flat 4 or *fa* and count down lines and spaces to 1 or *do*.
2. Look at the last note of the song, the "key" note. Is it where you found 1, *do*? If so, the song is in major. Is it on the line below 1, *do* (when 1, *do*, is on a line) or in the space below 1, *do,* (when 1, *do,* is in a space)? If so, the song is in minor.

Not all scales are major or minor. After all, scales came after songs. They are simply an ordering of the pitches used in music. Some songs have only five notes— their scales are *penta-tonic*; some use only three tones—their scales are *tri-tonic*. Some eight-tone scales sound very different from the usual major and minor; they are modes known as Mixolydian, Phrygian, Dorian and so on.[2] But for most music of North America, an understanding of basic major and minor scales will suffice.

INTERVALS; MELODIC TURNS AND PATTERNS

Intervals

THE DISTANCE FROM ONE PITCH TO ANOTHER IS CALLED AN *INTERVAL*. The interval is named first for its size, counting the lower note as 1 and counting each scale step to, and including, the higher note. The interval from C to G is a *fifth*:

[2]For a more complete discussion of these other scale systems, see Lois Choksy, *The Kodály Method*, 2nd ed. (Englewood Cliffs, N.J.: Prentice-Hall, 1988).

```
G  5
F  4
E  3
D  2
C  1
```

The interval from C to E is a *third:*

```
E  3
D  2
C  1
```

However, the interval from E to G also is a third:

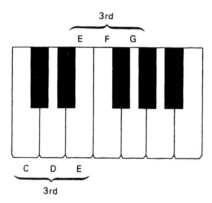

EXAMPLE 35

Yet, one can see that these two "thirds" are not the same *size* intervals—C to E is two whole steps, while E to G is only a half step and a whole step. The first is a bigger third, the second a smaller one. To distinguish between these two sizes of thirds, we use the word *major* for the bigger interval and the word *minor* for the smaller interval. Thirds may be either major (two whole steps) or minor (a step and a half).

The chorus to "Skip to My Lou" begins with thirds (Example 36), as do the opening notes of the "Star-Spangled Banner" (Example 37) and "O Canada" (Example 38).

EXAMPLE 36

EXAMPLE 37

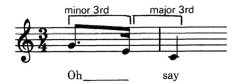

Oh_____ say

EXAMPLE 38

O   Ca - na - da

There also are *major* seconds and *minor* seconds in the scale:

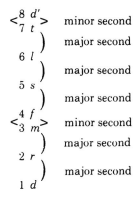

If we sing the first phrase of "Yankee Doodle," we will hear both major (bigger) and minor (smaller) seconds (Example 39). The familiar tune of "Old Hundredth" ("Praise God from Whom All Blessings Flow") is constructed almost entirely of major and minor seconds (Example 40).

EXAMPLE 39

EXAMPLE 40

Fourths in our singing music are generally all the same size. They contain two whole steps and one half step:

8 *d'*
7 *t*
6 *l*
5 *s*
4 *f*
3 *m*
2 *r*
1 *d*

These are called *perfect* fourths rather than major or minor. Many songs begin with the interval of the perfect fourth (see Examples 41 and 42).

EXAMPLE 41 "Here Comes the Bride"

Here   comes   the   bride

EXAMPLE 42 "The Farmer in the Dell"

The   far – mer   in   the   dell ____

One fourth is not perfect. From 4 to 7 (*fa* to *ti*), there are only whole steps. This is a bigger fourth than the perfect fourth. It is called an *augmented fourth*:

7 *t*
6 *l*   Augmented fourth
5 *s*
4 *f*

It rarely occurs in songs.

Like fourths, fifths are called perfect. The perfect fifth occurs at the end of the children's song "Ring around the Rosy" (Example 43). It contains a major third and a minor third. Only one fifth is *not* perfect—the one from 7 *(ti)* to the 4' *(fa')* has *two* minor thirds. It is smaller than a perfect fifth; it is called a *diminished fifth*. It rarely occurs in songs.

EXAMPLE 43

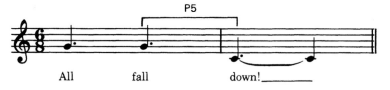

All   fall   down! _____

Sixths and sevenths, like seconds and thirds, are major and minor. If we invert (turn upside down) a major third, the result is a minor sixth (Example 44); if we invert a minor third, the result is a major sixth (Example 45).

EXAMPLE 44

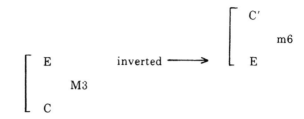

EXAMPLE 45

The "Mocking Bird" song begins with a major sixth, as does "My Bonnie" (Example 46).

EXAMPLE 46

Sevenths are inversions of seconds. If the second is major (C to D, *do* to *re*, for example), its inversion (D to C', *re* to high *do*) is a minor seventh. If the second is minor (E to F, *mi* to *fa*, for example), its inversion (F to E, *fa* to high *mi*) is a major seventh. Sevenths, major or minor, rarely occur in songs.

The eighth step above any note is its *octave*. The octave sounds "the same, but higher or lower." The last phrase of "Joy to the World" contains an octave leap (Example 47, p. 135).

Intervals and Tonal Function

Although the *size* of all major thirds or of all perfect fourths is the same, within a given key no two major thirds, perfect fourths, or other like-sized intervals actually

EXAMPLE 47

And   hea-ven,   and   hea – ven and   na – ture sing!

are the same. Some are much easier to sing than others. Low 5 to 1 (low *s* to *d*) is an extremely easy perfect fourth to sing. It occurs with great frequency at the beginning of songs and at the beginnings of phrases:

P4 . . . Here comes the bride,

P4 . . . The farmer in the dell

P4 . . . Down in the valley

On the other hand, the perfect fourth ascending from 2 to 5 (*r* to *s*) or descending from 5 to 2 (*s* to *r*) is generally difficult for people to sing in tune.

How can this be? They are, after all, both perfect fourths. Why should one be relatively easy to perform and the other somewhat difficult?

The answer lies in the *function* of specific tones within the tonal system. In the diatonic major scale, the individual pitches have certain tendencies—some more strongly than others. Try singing the major scale, stopping on the seventh step, *ti*. There is a strong urge to complete the scale, to push on to 8 (*do*). The seventh scale degree is referred to as the *leading tone* because of this tendency. Its primary *function* in melodies is to lead us to the keynote or tonal center.

Start singing a descending pattern on the 5 (*so*). When you reach 4 (*fa*), what seems the next most natural pitch? 3 (*mi*). The fourth scale step has a melodic tendency to fall to the third.

Not all notes have as strong or well-defined directional tendencies as 4 (*fa*) and 7 (*ti*), but some scale steps *are* stronger and others weaker. The fifth scale degree, *so*, is a pivot point in melodies—it frequently functions as the halfway mark in songs, the so-called *half-cadence* or end of a question phrase.

The sixth scale degree has no specific directional tendency and, often, no strong cadential role.[3] Its function is less specific.

The second scale degree *(re)*, like the fifth degree *(so)*, often plays an important role in half-cadences and cadences (endings). Because of these varied roles that notes play within a tonal system, tonal function has more to do with melody than do intervals. It does not help much to know the sound of the perfect fourth from low 5 (low *so*) to 1 (*do*) in "Here Comes the Bride" when the fourth we are asked to sing is from 3 to 6. It *feels* like a totally different interval.

For this reason, perhaps, it could be more useful to study melodic characteristics through *melodic turns* and *patterns* rather than through intervals.

Melodic Turns and Patterns

While every melody is made up of intervals one after the other, it is the grouping of those intervals into melodic turns and patterns that makes some melodies easier to remember than others. There are certain melodic turns and patterns that seem characteristic of English-language songs. They are part of the culture: the taunting chant of young children (Example 48) and its rhythmic variation (Example 49); the many tunes that begin or end with a 3-2-1 (*m-r-d*) or a 5-4-3-2-1 (*s-f-m-r-d*), shown in

---

[3]The sixth degree can hold a strong cadential position in the so-called deceptive cadence, where it is substituted for the chord on 1, the tonic.

Examples 50 and 51; and the many others that approach the ending of a song by starting a fourth below the keynote and moving stepwise to it—for instance, Example 52.

EXAMPLE 48

Na – na – na – na – na – na!
Ring   a – round   the   ro –   sy,

EXAMPLE 49

I   am   big – ger than   you   are!

EXAMPLE 50

Three   blind   mice

EXAMPLE 51

Mer – ri – ly,   mer – ri – ly,   mer – ri – ly, mer – ri – ly,

Life   is   but   a   dream! _____

EXAMPLE 52

Stuck a feather in his cap and called

it   mac – a – ro – ni!

Here we go 'round the mulberry bush so early

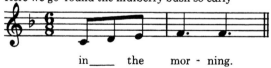

in ____ the   mor – ning.

A melodic turn that occurs often at the beginning or in the middle of tunes is 1, low 6, low 5 (*do,* low *la,* low *so*)—see Example 53.

EXAMPLE 53

I saw the light

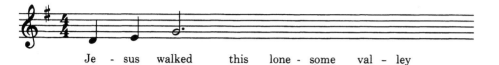

Je - sus walked this lone - some val - ley

Swing low, sweet char - i - ot_____

There's a hole in my buck - et, dear Li - za, dear Li - za

Another common pattern is built on 1-3 and 5 (*do-mi* and *so*) ascending or descending, with the occasional use of the octave 8 (high *do*) or the low 5 (low *so*)—see Example 54.

EXAMPLE 54

Lou, Lou, skip to my Lou

Oh___ say can you see

I'm going to leave_____ (old Tex - as now)

Oh, my dar - ling, oh, my dar - ling, oh, my dar - ling (Clem-en-tine!)

Although there is no quick way to learn music reading, the serious student would be well advised to learn these very common patterns and to look for them in songs. They are frequently there, thinly disguised by rhythmic variation.

To review, the patterns are given in the following list in the key of F without rhythmic variation; of course, in real melodies they may occur in any key and may have great rhythmic variation.

1. The children's chant:

   s   s   m   l   s   m

2. The 3-2-1 and 5-4-3-2-1 song endings:

      m   r   d   s   f   m   r   d

3. The song ending on 5-6-7-8, approaching from below the tonal center or keynote:

   s₁   l₁   t₁   d

4. The melodic turn on 1 (*do*), low 5 (low *so*), and low 6 (low *la*):

   d   l₁   s₁   s₁   l₁   d

5. Patterns built on 1-3-5-8 (*d-m-s-d'*) or on low 5-1-3-5 (low *s-d-m-s*):

   d   m   s   s   m   d   s₁   d   m   s   d   m   s   d'

There are certainly many tonal patterns and melodic turns other than the five groups suggested here for study. However, the latter are among the most frequent in English-language songs. They are essentially a part of our melodic idiom. To know them is to make both singing and music reading easier.

Which of these five patterns occur in the New England game song shown in Example 55? Patterns 4 and 5 each occur *five* times in this song. Pattern 1 (*s-l-s*) occurs once and 2 (*m-r-d*) twice. The song contains no other melodic elements. This song is not particularly unusual. It is representative of a great many North American folksongs and singing games.

Let us examine another one (Example 56). It contains pattern 5 three times and 3 once.

EXAMPLE 55 "I've Been to Haarlem"

I've been to Haar - lem, I've been to Do - ver,

I've tra - veled this wide world all o - ver; O - ver, o - ver,

three times o - ver, Drink all the brand - y - wine and

turn the glass - es o - ver. Sail - ing east, Sail - ing west,

Sail - ing o - ver the o - cean, Bet - ter watch out when the

boat be - gins to rock or you'll lose your girl in the o - cean!

EXAMPLE 56 "Here We Go 'Round the Mulberry Bush"

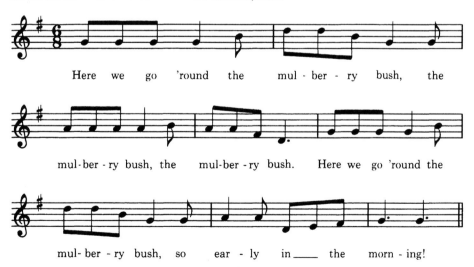

Here we go 'round the mul - ber - ry bush, the

mul - ber - ry bush, the mul - ber - ry bush. Here we go 'round the

mul - ber - ry bush, so ear - ly in ___ the morn - ing!

Sequence in Melody

One other melodic aspect is common to numerous songs. WHEN A MELODIC *PATTERN* IS REPEATED, BUT AT A HIGHER OR LOWER PLACE, THAT REPETITION IS REFERRED TO AS A *SEQUENCE*. The melodic contour is the same, but the higher or lower placement gives the tune more variety than an exact repetition would. See Examples 57 and 58.

EXAMPLE 57   Contour of an exact repetition

Are   you   sleep - ing,

EXAMPLE 58   Contour of a repetition in sequence

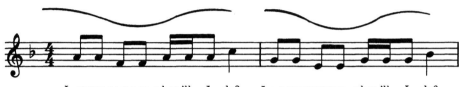

Lost my part-ner, what 'll   I   do?   Lost my part-ner, what 'll   I   do?

Many songs built around the five patterns given earlier extend and vary those patterns by use of sequence.

SUMMARY

Melodies are made up of patterns of higher, lower, and repeated pitches. Each melody has a contour or shape, and most have a middle point that sounds incomplete (half-cadence) and an ending that has a feeling of completeness or closure (cadence).

If one arranges all the pitches in a melody in ascending or descending order, the result is a scale. Scales may be major (with two whole steps at the beginning) or minor (with one and one-half steps at the beginning).

Key signatures indicate which notes must be sharped or flatted to produce the major-scale pattern or the minor-scale pattern. By looking at the key signature and the last note of a song, we can determine whether the song is major or minor and in what key the song is.

The distance between two notes is called an interval; there are major, minor, perfect, augmented, and diminished intervals.

Certain note groupings, melodic turns or patterns, appear to be characteristic of English-language songs. Familiarity with these can lead to easier music reading, singing, and playing.

ACTIVITIES

1. In a school music series book, locate songs with the following key signatures: two sharps, three sharps, four sharps; one flat, two flats, three flats. Tell where *do* or 1 is in each, whether the song is major or minor, and why you think it is major or minor.

2. Choose one song from a school music series text. Find all the different notes in it and arrange them on a staff from lowest to highest. Is it a complete scale? If so, is it major or minor? If not, which notes are missing, and can you tell by the notes present in the song whether it is of major or minor character? How can you tell?

3. In a school music series, locate each of the five melodic patterns given on p. 138. You may find five separate songs or more than one pattern in one song.

SIMULTANEOUS SOUNDS

Monophonic Music

Thus far in this chapter, we have dealt with only the unaccompanied melody. Such a melody is called *monophonic*. Monophony was the predominant style of early music and is still the style of much of the folk music of the world. In monophonic music, only one musical line occurs. There is only melody.

Polyphonic Music

This is music in which two or more musical lines occur simultaneously. Each is a melody. Each can stand alone. The music is linear, but the effect of the lines sounding together is one of harmony. A simple example of two musical lines occurring together is the descant (Example 59).

EXAMPLE 59 Descant

Canons and rounds are other linear organizations of sound that produce harmonies (Example 60). Canonic melodic imitation can happen at the unison or at different pitch levels (Example 61).

EXAMPLE 60 Canon

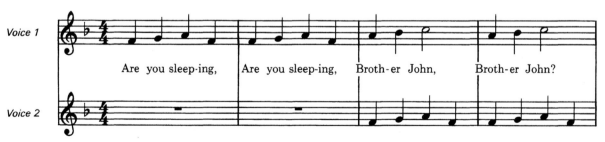

EXAMPLE 61   Canon at the fifth and the octave

Polyphony occurs in Bach fugues and inventions but may be found in music of every period from the Baroque to the twentieth century. Example 62 shows a polyphonic composition by Bach. Note that the lower voice performs the same melody as the upper but enters later and a fourth lower. The individual intervals formed in the process sound good together. They have a quality of consonance.

EXAMPLE 62   Bach: Duet from Cantata No. 78

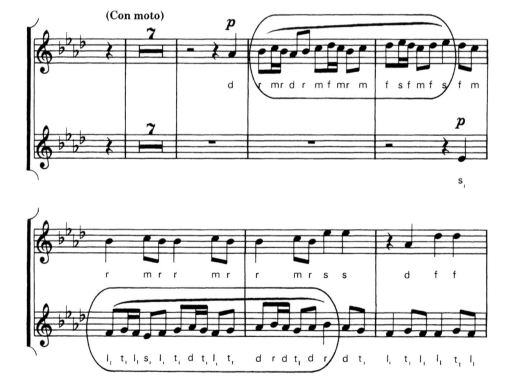

Dissonance caused by notes that do not sound exactly "right" together also occurs in polyphonic music. The dissonance creates tension in the music. When the dissonant intervals resolve to a consonant one, there is a feeling of release, of having arrived.

ACTIVITIES

1. Listen to a recording of a Gregorian chant. Is this music monophonic or polyphonic?
2. Listen to the Fugue in D Minor by J. S. Bach. Is this music monophonic or polyphonic? How many instances of dissonance can you hear in it?

Homophonic Music

In some music, one voice has the melody and other voices simply accompany that melody with a chordal accompaniment. This is called *homophony*. Church hymns are a clear example of homophony. A folksong accompanied by guitar chording is another example of homophonic music. Most popular music is homophonic.

Conclusion

In historic terms, monophony—unaccompanied melody—came first; later, to make the music more interesting, other melodies were added and polyphony was created. Last on the scene historically was homophony, melody with chordal accompaniment.

Both polyphonic and homophonic music employ consonance and dissonance to create tension and release, to make the melodies more interesting.

ACTIVITIES

1. Locate one example each of monophonic, polyphonic, and homophonic music to play for the class.
2. Find a simple folksong. Describe how it could be performed in a monophonic style; polyphonic style; homophonic style.

CHAPTER 11

FORM
The Architecture of Music
TEMPO, DYNAMICS AND TIMBRE
The Expressive Elements

FORM: THE ARCHITECTURE OF MUSIC

If you were to design or build a house, some aspects of it would be the same (two windows side-by-side would probably be the same size and shape). Some would be different (in one place you might choose to place a door rather than a window) and others would be similar (you might want a window, but perhaps a picture window rather than one of the same size and shape as the others).

You would design some aspects to be the same and some to be similar to give your house a unified appearance, but you would probably design some aspects to be different, for variety.

The principles of unity and variety are as applicable to music as to architecture; THE QUALITIES OF SAME, DIFFERENT, AND SIMILAR ARE USED IN MUSIC TO ACHIEVE UNITY AND VARIETY, much as they are in designing a house.

THE SMALLEST COMPLETE MUSICAL BUILDING BLOCK IS THE *PATTERN* OR *MOTIF*. This can consist of as few as three or four notes, as in the opening of Beethoven's Fifth Symphony (Example 1).

EXAMPLE 1

PATTERNS CAN BE SHORT PHRASES (Example 2) or MAY BE PUT TOGETHER TO MAKE LONGER PHRASES (Example 3).

EXAMPLE 2

Rain,   rain,   go a - way,

EXAMPLE 3

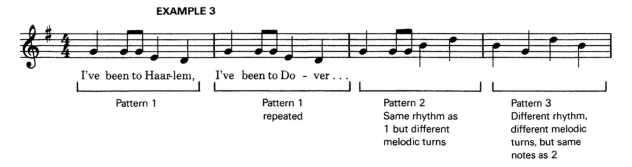

PHRASE ENDINGS SUGGEST BREATHING PLACES OR ARTICULATION POINTS IN MUSIC. Sometimes, but not always, the words in a song indicate the musical phrase endings; a comma, a question mark, an exclamation point, or a period in the text frequently coincides with the end of a musical phrase (Example 4).

EXAMPLE 4

However, not all music has words. Instrumental music is constructed by pattern and phrase just as songs are. Phrase endings in nonvocal music can be recognized as the places implying a momentary resting point. They have a feeling of pause, however brief that pause may actually be in terms of rhythmic value. One of the author's young students once defined phrase as "the place where the music breathes"—not a particularly scientific definition but certainly a highly descriptive one.

PHRASES IN MUSIC CAN BE EXACTLY THE SAME:

EXAMPLE 5

Are you sleep-ing,
Are you sleep-ing,

EXAMPLE 6

Ring a-round the ro-sy,
Pock-et full of po-sy,

or THEY CAN BE TOTALLY DIFFERENT:

EXAMPLE 7

The mon - key said 'twas all __ in fun, Pop goes the wea - sel!

We use letters of the alphabet to describe form, with the first phrase always designated as *a*. Examine the song "Hot Cross Buns" (Example 8). Which phrases are the same? Which are different? The first, second, and fourth are alike; the third is different. If we call the first phrase and all others like it *a* and the one different phrase *b*, the song is described as being in *aaba* form. An *aaba* form is found in many songs and many instrumental pieces.

EXAMPLE 8

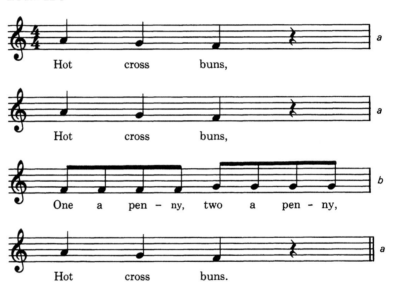

What would be the form of "Ring around the Rosy" (Example 9)?

EXAMPLE 9

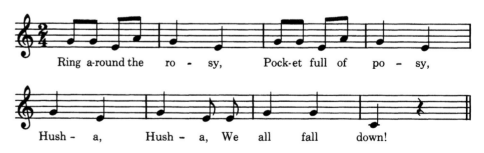

SOMETIMES, PHRASES ARE NOT EXACTLY ALIKE BUT THEY ARE NOT VERY DIFFERENT; THEY ARE SIMILAR (Example 10).

EXAMPLE 10

Flies in the but-ter-milk, shoo, fly, shoo! Flies in the but-ter-milk, shoo, fly, shoo!

In "Skip to My Lou," the second phrase is like the first except that it is a step lower. We cannot label this phrase a *b* because it is too similar to the first phrase. It is clearly an *a*. To show that it is different in some way from the *a* of the first phrase, we can put a 1 beside it: a^1. The form of this piece then would be diagramed as aa^1ab, indicating that only the last phrase (Example 11) is really "different."

EXAMPLE 11

Skip   to my Lou, my   dar -   ling!

Similar phrases sometimes differ in only the last notes: The first phrase ends on a note other than 1, *do*, and has a feeling of incompleteness; the second ends on the keynote (1, *do*) and produces a feeling of completeness. These kinds of phrases are referred to as *question phrases* (incomplete) and *answer phrases* (complete) (Example 12).

EXAMPLE 12

Do,   do,   do,   do,   do re-mem-ber   me,

Do,   do,   do,   do,   do re-mem-ber   me!

Question phrases and answer phrases do not have to be similar. When they are very different, they are labeled with different letters, *ab* (Example 13).

EXAMPLE 13

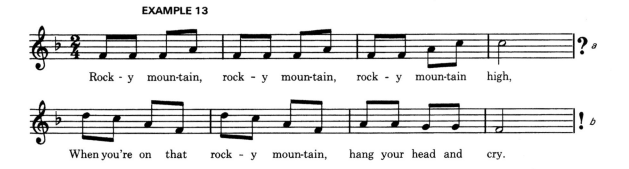

Rock - y moun-tain, rock - y moun-tain, rock - y moun-tain high,

When you're on that   rock - y moun-tain, hang your head and cry.

Sections

Just as a simple four-phrase song may be diagramed using alphabet letters to indicate which phrases are the same, which different, and which similar, larger works may be analyzed to discover which parts are the same, different, and similar. Let us first look at and listen to a more complex song, one with a verse and a chorus (Example 14).

EXAMPLE 14   "Greensleeves"

If we diagram the phrases of this song as we did the earlier ones, we see that the form of the verse is *abac*; the form of the refrain is *dedc*. However, if we look at the whole first section and label it *A* and the second section and label it *B*, we have an overall form of *AB* . This is a common form in larger works.

Listen to the third movement, Minuet and Trio, of the Mozart Symphony No. 39 in E-flat Major. The three sections, *ABA*, are clearly distinguishable; within the *A* section, there are phrases that could be labeled *a*'s and *b*'s, and within the second section, there are phrases that could be labeled *c*'s and *d*'s, so that when we diagram by section, the final form could be shown as *AABA*.

ACTIVITIES

1. Find examples in a school music series of songs in *aaba* and *aabc* forms. Find one example of a song with sequence. Analyze and diagram the form of the song. Find one with a question phrase and an answer phrase. Analyze and diagram its form.
2. Compose two rhythm phrases, each eight beats long in $\frac{4}{4}$ meter. Arrange your phrases into *aaba* form. (You should now have a four-phrase, 32-beat rhythm composition.)
3. As you listen to music on radio, television, tapes, and so on, try to determine where phrase endings are and which phrases in the music are the same, which different, and which similar.

Larger Forms

While there are many types of musical compositions—symphonies, operas, popular music, suites, chamber music, oratorios, solo instrumental works, to name only a few—there are not very many specific and unique large forms. In general, they can probably be reduced to eight:

- Rondo
- Theme and variations
- Minuet and trio
- Dance forms
- Ritornello
- Passacaglia
- Fugue
- Sonata

Most other forms are simply combinations or mutations of these.

Since the effective teaching of music listening will depend to some extent on the teacher's ability to recognize at least some of these forms, a brief description of each is given, with some suggested musical examples for listening.

Rondo

Perhaps the simplest of all musical forms is the rondo. A basic tune (theme) is given first. Then, a second tune is introduced. At the end of the second tune, we return to the first tune. Then, a third tune is introduced, after which we return again to the first. It is like a many-layered sandwich, with bread at the top and bottom and in between each layer. Rondo form may be diagramed as *ABACADA* and coda. The coda is a fancy ending usually made up of bits of the *A* theme. A clear example of rondo form may be heard in the Haydn Cello Concerto in D Major, Op. 101, third movement.

Theme and Variations

Like rondo form, the theme-and-variations form is generally an easy one to detect. First, a tune is presented in its entirety. Often, this tune is not even by the composer; it is frequently one known by many people, a somewhat "popular" tune. The composer first reminds us of how the original tune goes; then, he or she changes it in a series of restatements. The tune may be changed from major to minor in one variation; it may be altered rhythmically in another variation; it may appear in the bass in another; in still another, it may be upside down or backwards. However, it is always there in some form in every variation.

A good example of this form for listening is Mozart's *Theme and Variations on "Ah, Vous Dirai-je Maman"* ("Twinkle, Twinkle, Little Star"). Another is the set of variations composed by Beethoven on "God Save the Queen" ("My Country, 'Tis of Thee").

Minuet-and-Trio form has been discussed earlier, under Sections (p. 149). This *ABA* form may be found in the third movement of most symphonies of Mozart and Haydn, and it evolved into the ¾ waltzlike third movements found in the later Beethoven and Brahms symphonies.

Dance Forms

This is not one form but a series of forms descended from actual dances of the Renaissance. Each has its own special characteristics and internal form. They are allemandes and gigues and courantes—all dances, some stately, others lively. They are listed here together because they were put together by composers like Bach and Handel to form *suites*. They became the general pattern for suites followed by composers for two centuries. A good suite for listening is *Music for the Royal Fireworks* by George Frideric Handel.

Ritornello

Ritornello is another form much used by the Baroque composers Handel and Bach and their contemporaries. The word *ritornello* is Italian for "returning," and return is what it does, time after time. The *A* theme returns frequently, alternating with other themes. How, then, is it different from rondo form? It is different in the instrumentation. In ritornello form, the whole orchestra plays the *A* theme while a smaller group of instruments plays the other, alternating, themes. This form is the grandfather of the solo instrumental concerto (the piano concerto, the violin concerto, and so on). It includes a *cadenza* near the end—a place for the soloists to show their virtuosity. The orchestra stops playing and the soloists may take off in instrumental flights of fancy. In olden days, the composer did not write cadenzas; they were left to the imagination of the performer.

A clear example of ritornello form with a cadenza (performed by harpsichord in this case) is Bach's *Brandenburg Concerto* No. 5.

Passacaglia

Passacaglia is another very old form, still used by composers in the twentieth century. Like theme and variations, it first presents a tune and then offers variations on that tune. However, it is different in that the theme is in the bass, always in ¾ meter, and always exactly eight measures long. Each variation that follows is over that same bass line and must also be exactly eight measures long. The constant repetition of the bass theme makes passacaglias very easy to follow aurally.

A clear example of passacaglia form may be heard in Bach's Passacaglia in C Minor. A later and somewhat freer passacaglia form is employed by Brahms in the fourth movement of his Symphony No. 4 in E Minor.

Fugue

Fugue, another form brought to its highest point in the Baroque period but still used today, is based on overlapping imitative theme statements. A theme is stated completely in one key. Then it is stated repeatedly in different places—the first scale degree, the fifth scale degree, the octave. It is stated in higher places and in lower places. Meanwhile, a second tune, a *countermelody* is played against it.

An easy fugue theme to follow is Bach's Little Fugue in G Minor.

Sonata

The most complex of these "basic" forms is sonata form. It is the form used in many solo instrumental works and in first movements of symphonies. In sonata form, two main musical ideas are presented (*exposition*), then elaborated upon (*development*), and finally returned to (*recapitulation*).

The first movement of the Symphony No. 5 by Schubert is an example of sonata form.

Summary

Music has patterns and motifs. These may be short phrases or may be combined in longer phrases. Phrases are breathing places or articulation points in music. In songs, phrase endings frequently coincide with punctuation marks in the text, but they do not always do so.

Phrases in a song or another piece of music can be the same, different, or similar. Similar phrases may consist of melodic sequences. Similar phrases may end on different notes, making one of them feel incomplete (question phrase) and the other feel complete (answer phrase). Short forms like songs may be diagramed with lowercase alphabet letters (*aabc*).

In larger works, same, different, and similar phrases are organized into sections. Sections may be diagramed with uppercase letters to show the patterns of their occurrence and recurrence (*ABA*).

While there are many larger forms, certain forms are fairly basic and in combinations and mutations have provided patterns for the organizations of music for over three centuries. These forms are dance forms, passacaglia, fugue, ritornello, rondo, theme and variations, minuet and trio, and sonata.

ACTIVITIES

1. In the music section of your library, find and listen to the following works:
    a. J. S. Bach, Little Fugue in G Minor (fugue)
    b. J. S. Bach, Passacaglia in C Minor (passacaglia)
    c. J. S. Bach, *Brandenburg Concerto* No. 5 (ritornello)
    d. George Frideric Handel, *The Royal Fireworks* Suite (dance forms)
    e. Franz Joseph Haydn, Cello Concerto in D Major, Op. 101 (rondo)
    f. W. A. Mozart, *Theme and Variations on "Ah, Vous Dirai-je Maman"* (theme and variations)
    g. Franz Schubert, Symphony No. 5, first movement (sonata)
    h. W. A. Mozart, Symphony No. 39 in E-flat Major, third movement (minuet and trio)
2. Choose part of one of the above and chart its sections with *A*'s, *B*'s, *C*'s and so on.
3. Compose a rhythm pattern eight measures long in $\frac{2}{4}$ meter. Get together with four classmates. Organize your five compositions into one, in rondo form. Together, compose a coda reminiscent of bits of the *A* pattern but not exactly repeating that pattern.

TEMPO, DYNAMICS, AND TIMBRE: THE EXPRESSIVE ELEMENTS

As form is used to create unity and variety in musical works, so also are tempo, dynamics, and timbre—the expressive elements—used.

Tempo

TEMPO IS THE SPEED AT WHICH THE BEAT MOVES. In a song, the words often suggest what tempo might be suitable. A lullaby would probably be sung slowly, in a rocking tempo; a singing game would be sung faster, in a skipping or running tempo; a ballad telling an unhappy tale, more slowly; a song with a refrain of nonsense syllables (doo-dahs or fa-las) in a faster tempo. GENERALLY, THE TEMPO, ONCE ESTABLISHED, REMAINS THE SAME THROUGHOUT A SONG, ALTHOUGH IT CAN BE SLOWED DOWN OR SPEEDED UP TO EMPHASIZE THE MEANING OF PARTICULAR PHRASES OR VERSES. This is simply a matter of performance style. IN LARGER FORMS, TEMPO CAN CHANGE WITHIN A SECTION OR FROM ONE SECTION TO ANOTHER. Composers use tempo changes as a way of creating interest. A consistent steady tempo, such as that found in a movement of a Handel suite, gives the piece a sense of unity. A quickening tempo, such as Wagner's "The Ride of the Valkyries," creates variety and excitement.

TEMPO CHANGES MAY BE GRADUAL (Ravel's "Bolero") OR SUDDEN (Schubert's "Gretchen am Spinnrade"). Although some composers have been very specific about the tempo at which they want compositions performed, even giving metronome markings, some others have given only the most general indication by the use of tempo terms. Some music has no indications of the desired tempo. In both these later cases, tempo becomes a variable open to interpretation by performers.

Some terms generally associated with tempo are[1]

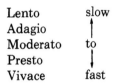

Lento	slow
Adagio	↑
Moderato	to
Presto	↓
Vivace	fast

Dynamics

DYNAMICS REFERS TO THE RELATIVE SOFTNESS OR LOUDNESS OF MUSIC. As the character of a melody and text suggests an appropriate tempo for a song, so it suggests an appropriate dynamic level. A lullaby would naturally be sung more softly, a marching song more loudly.

WITHIN LARGER FORMS, DYNAMICS ARE USED TO CREATE UNITY AND VARIETY. In music of the Baroque period (Bach, Handel), the dynamic level rarely varies within a given section but does contrast from section to section. Later composers (Schubert, Beethoven, Brahms) use dynamic changes within sections to create variety, drama, and interest.

DYNAMIC CHANGES MAY OCCUR GRADUALLY (Copland, *Appalachian Spring*, "Simple Gifts" theme) OR SUDDENLY (Beethoven, Symphony No. 9, fourth movement, Chorale).

Like tempo indications, dynamic markings were relatively uncommon in music before the nineteenth century. Even where dynamic markings are very specific, they are open to interpretation by performers. How loud is "very loud"? "medium loud"? "softer"? Each conductor and performer has his or her own idea.

[1]Italian is the universal language of music.

The commonly used terms for dynamics are

- *piano* (soft), indicated in music by the lowercase letter *p*
- *forte* (loud), indicated in music by the lowercase letter *f*

There are a number of modifications and extensions possible with these two symbols. First is the word *mezzo* ("medium") attached to each:

- *mezzo forte—mf* (medium loud)
- *mezzo piano—mp* (medium soft)

This gives us four relative dynamic levels—five, if we consider that there must be one in the middle that is just a normal level, neither medium loud nor medium soft. Then there are increasing numbers of *p*'s and *f*'s possible to indicate softer and louder (*pp, ff*), much softer or louder (*ppp, fff*), and very, very soft or loud (*pppp, ffff*).

When composers wish a place in the music to begin at a softer level and build gradually to a louder one, they use the crescendo mark: ⟨ .

When they wish a place in the music to begin at a louder level and gradually become softer, they use a decrescendo mark (also known as a *diminuendo*): ⟩ .

If they want a suddenly louder or softer effect, they use a *subito forte* or *subito piano: sf* or *sp*.

Through the use of dynamics, composers make music more expressive.

Timbre

TIMBRE IS THE MUSICAL TERM FOR THE QUALITY OF MUSICAL SOUND. It is also referred to as tone color. Both voices and instruments possess timbre. It is this quality that makes it possible to distinguish one singer from another, even if they have the same type voice and sing in the same range. It is this quality that enables us to distinguish the sound of one instrument from the sound of another when the two are playing the same notes.

TIMBRE IS DEPENDENT UPON THE SIZE AND SHAPE OF THE INSTRUMENT PRODUCING THE SOUND, THE MATERIAL OF WHICH IT IS MADE, AND THE WAY IN WHICH THE SOUND IS PRODUCED. In singers, two voices with the same range are still distinguishable because the vocal chords may be of different sizes, the resonating cavities of the singers will be different, the lung capacity may vary, and the use of breath may not be the same. The result is the often indefinable difference in sound we call timbre.

In instruments, it is easier to see why sound qualities differ. There are woody sounds, made by instruments with wooden reeds in the mouthpiece—oboe, clarinet, English horn, bassoon. There are brass sounds—trumpets, French horns, trombones, tubas. There are string sounds—violins, violas, cellos, basses. Finally, there are percussion sounds —timpani, drums, gongs, and so on. Within each family— woodwinds, brasses, strings, percussion—there are similarities in timbre. From family to family, there are noticeable differences in timbre.

Composers often use timbre to vary a repeated theme. In the opening section of the fourth movement of his Symphony No. 9, Beethoven has the chorale theme stated first by the double basses, next by the rest of the string family, then by the woodwinds, and finally by the brasses and percussion, layering timbre upon timbre to build excitement and interest.

Timbre is a more subtle musical material than tempo or dynamics, but, like tempo and dynamics, it contributes to the expressive qualities of music.

Woodwinds: Flute, Oboe, Clarinet, Bassoon. *Students from the Intermediate and Youth orchestras of the Mount Royal Conservatory, Calgary.*

Brasses: Trumpet, French Horn, Trombone, Tuba. *Students from the Intermediate and Youth orchestras of the Mount Royal Conservatory, Calgary.*

Strings: Violin, Viola, Cello, Bass Viol. *Students from the Intermediate and Youth orchestras of the Mount Royal Conservatory, Calgary.*

Percussion: Marimba. *Student from the Youth Orchestra of the Mount Royal Conservatory, Calgary.*

Percussion: Timpani. *Student from the Youth Orchestra of the Mount Royal Conservatory, Calgary.*

Summary

Tempo (the relative fastness or slowness of the beat), dynamics (the relative loudness or softness of the music), and timbre (the vocal and instrumental tone colors employed) add expressiveness to music

ACTIVITIES

1. In a school music series, find examples of tempo and dynamic markings.

2. Choose a song without tempo or dynamic indications. Write in traditional tempo and dynamic markings to make the piece more interesting. Use a crescendo or a decrescendo at some point in the song. Perform it following the markings you have used.

3. Take the rhythm rondo you composed with other students (p. 151). With your group, add tempo and dynamic indications to it. Orchestrate it in a way that will create varied timbres. Use rhythm instruments, hand clapping, foot stamping, voice sounds, or any other rhythmic sound-producing mechanism to create timbral variety. Have your group perform their finished composition for the class.

CHAPTER 12

SO YOU WANT TO TEACH MUSIC
Putting It All Together

How is it possible to teach a subject as vast as music to children? Obviously, it is not possible to teach everything about music in the six years of elementary school (or even the seventy or eighty years of one life span)! Choices must be made, and those choices should not be arbitrary. There must be a basis for curriculum choices if anything of educational value is to occur in the music class. That basis is ultimately the individual teacher's philosophy regarding music education and overall goals as they relate to that philosophy.

Philosophy and *goals* are words that tend to frighten beginning teachers. Let us attempt to demystify them.

A PHILOSOPHY FOR TEACHING

Phi-los-o-phy, *n.* The love or pursuit of wisdom; i.e., the search for basic principles. Systematized principles of any subject or branch of knowledge.[1]

Philosophy, *n.* Love of wisdom or knowledge, especially that which deals with . . . the most general causes and principles of things.[2]

Phi-los-o-phy, *n.* Study of the basic principles of a particular field of knowledge; practical wisdom that comes from knowledge of general laws and principles; system of general beliefs or views.[3]

What do you believe about music education? What do you see as the "basic principles," the "general causes of things"? What do you think should be the "basic principles" or the "system of general beliefs" about music education?

---

[1]*Larousse Illustrated International Encyclopedia and Dictionary,* McGraw-Hill International Book Co., New York: Librairie Larousse S.A., Paris, 1972.

[2]*The Concise Oxford Dictionary of Current English,* 4th ed. ed., H. W. Fowler and F. G. Fowler, (rev. by E. McIntosh), The Clarendon Press, Oxford, 1956.

[3]*The Scribner-Bantam English Dictionary,* E. B. Williams (Gen. Ed.), Bantam Books, Inc., New York, 1979.

That it should be equally available to everyone?

That it contributes to human development in areas not as well served by many other subjects and should therefore have a prominent place in curriculum?

That the quality of music used in teaching will influence children's ability to make knowledgeable choices in later life?

That any musical material may be used to teach musical skills or to lead to musical understandings?

That it is important to begin with a music that is suitable to the child's age and that is drawn from the child's culture?

That music of all cultures, periods, and genres is suitable for use in teaching children of any age?

That music instruction should occupy an important place in early childhood programs?

That informal sing-alongs are sufficient for the early school years and that formal music classes should begin with the junior high band?

That the child's voice is the best instrument for early education?

That children learn music more readily through instrumental experience?

That movement and dance are important to musical development?

That musical literacy is a desirable aim of music education?

That the musical experience is all-important and that literacy is not a necessary facet of that experience?

That children should be given opportunities to create music?

That composition and improvisation are best left to people more knowledgeable in music?

That music is a subject in its own right, with a body of knowledge to be imparted, and for that reason should occupy its own time in scheduling?

That music as one of the "fine arts" should be integrated into a "fine arts curriculum"?

That the best use of music in the elementary school is as an enrichment to other subject areas (for example, social studies)?

The foregoing are all statements of a philosophic nature. They all express currently held beliefs about the teaching of music. It is obvious that there are many contradictions among them. All, however, may be found in curriculum practice and in written curricula in North America. In some instances, they are merely implied by the curriculum choices made in districts, while in others, they are specifically stated in guides.

The individual teacher should examine his or her own beliefs about music education and not simply unquestioningly accept those imposed by tradition or authority. Curriculum guides, once written, notoriously sit on shelves gathering dust and are pulled out only every five years or so for "revision." It has been the author's experience that no effective music teacher with a well-planned program of instruction was ever fired for not "following the guide."

ACTIVITIES

1. Write a paper detailing what you believe music education should be—that is, your own "philosophy" of music education. You may draw on any of the suggestions in this chapter, but you may also include ideas not given here.

2. Examine a copy of a music curriculum guide for your district, county, state, or province. Answer the following questions about it:

Does it have a page or pages called philosophy? If so, compare that philosophy with your own. In what ways is it the same? different?

If there is no page labeled "philosophy," do the activities and curriculum choices imply certain beliefs? If so, which? How do these compare with your own?

GOALS

Setting Goals

If one starts out aimlessly on a Sunday drive, one may have a good time but will probably return home without having "gotten anyplace." Conversely, if one wishes to get from Baltimore to New York, one would probably not drive "aimlessly." There is a goal, New York, and the route taken should logically lead from Baltimore to New York. The road to Washington is perhaps prettier or more fun, but if the goal is New York, the Washington road won't get one there.

Goals in education are similar. They are "where we want to get to," and they are related directly to the philosophy we hold. If our philosophy places importance on musical literacy, then one of our goals must be "to make the traditional language of music known to children; to develop competency with musical reading and writing." An "aimless" musical curriculum is unlikely to result in the achievement of that goal.

Each statement of philosophy should have a related goal. Without that goal, we are left with high-sounding phrases that go nowhere.

ACTIVITIES

Write a goal statement for each of your statements of philosophy.

Achieving Curriculum Goals

Once a philosophy has been stated and goals through which to implement philosophy have been set, it is possible to begin to make the kinds of curriculum choices through which those goals can be met.

Perhaps, some statements of philosophy and goals are not achievable within the framework of a specific school or school system. If, for example, one believes strongly that music should be of equal importance to mathematics and reading in curriculum but the school system dictates that only an hour and a half be allotted weekly to music, the curriculum design will have to be achievable within that ninety minutes a week. That does not mean that one should alter either philosophy or goals, but simply that to achieve them, it will be necessary to work on committees at the policy-making level to try to influence decision making with regard to time allotment. This is not something that can be done in the first year of teaching, but if one believes strongly enough in a particular course of action and works toward that course of action, change will occur.

Skill Development and Concept Inference

Let us, however, examine goals that are not dependent on outside authority. If one goal is "to develop children's creative abilities in music," what can we do to work toward achieving that goal in first grade? third grade? sixth grade? How can we harness the activities through which children learn music—singing, playing, instruments, moving, listening, reading, writing, creating—to develop their creative skills? How can we deal with the elements of music—melody, duration, form, tempo, dynamics, timbre, simultaneous sounds—in such a way that children will hold the understandings necessary for creating within each or all of these elements?

Two types of learnings are necessary:

1. *Skill development.* The ability to sing, to play, to move, to listen, to read, to write, and to create must be fostered.
2. *Concept inference.*[4] Generalizations must be made and understandings must be arrived at about melody, duration, form, tempo, dynamics, timbre, and simultaneous sounds. These come as a result of the musical experiences. Concepts differ from facts in that a concept is a broad understanding that has application in many situations, while a fact is specific and immediate.

    Concept   PITCHES IN MELODIES MOVE HIGHER OR LOWER OR REPEAT.

    Fact   In "Yankee Doodle," the first note is repeated.

Both skills and concepts must be sequenced from the simplest and lowest level to the most complex, and children must be taught on the level at which they enter.[5]

In duration, for example, one beginning-level concept is

MOST MUSIC HAS A STEADY BEAT.

This can be taught at first grade by stepping the beat to "Ring around the Rosy," at third grade by tapping the beat while singing "Turn the Glasses Over," at sixth grade by conducting the beat while singing "Yankee Doodle." However, if the children in third grade or sixth grade have inferred the correct concept about beat in first grade, they can move to more complex activities involving the beat or to demonstrating beat in more sophisticated musical material:

At third grade, by moving to the beat of a compound-meter game ("The Noble Duke of York") and by determining "how many beats go by" in a phrase.

At sixth grade, by demonstrating with clapping the beats in an asymmetric meter, $\frac{5}{4}$ or $\frac{7}{8}$, accenting the correct places.

The concept inference is the same in all these experiences:

MOST MUSIC HAS A STEADY BEAT.

In this way, an easy, low-level concept may be applied at increasingly complex skill levels.

However, there are more complex understandings or concepts about duration:

OVER THE BEAT, MUSIC MOVES IN LONGER AND SHORTER SOUNDS AND SILENCES. THESE SOUNDS AND SILENCES MAY BE ARRANGED EVENLY OR UNEVENLY.

The first grader can step the beat and clap the rhythm to discover this concept. He or she can compare the "even" sounds over the beat in "Lucy Locket" (Example 1) with "uneven" arrangements of sound in "The Farmer in the Dell" (Example 2).

---

[4]Concept statements may be found in each chapter in Part II. They are printed in SMALL CAPITALS.

[5]See Lois Choksy, Robert M. Abramson, Avon E. Gillespie, and David Woods, *Teaching Music in the Twentieth Century* (Englewood Cliffs, N.J.: Prentice-Hall, Inc., 1986).

EXAMPLE 1

Lu – cy   Lock – et   lost   her   pock – et

EXAMPLE 2

The   far – mer   in   the   dell_____

The third grader can sing the song "Chairs to Mend," clap the ostinato (Example 3), and through this activity discover and note the uneven pattern in the music.

EXAMPLE 3

Chairs   to mend,   old   chairs   to mend

The sixth grader can augment or diminish known uneven rhythms ♩. ♪ and ♪♩♪ to ♩.♩ and ♩ ♩ ♩ to figure out how the new ones sound.

Thus, a complex concept may also be applied at many skill levels.

If one thinks of the elements of music as one side of a grid and the activities through which children learn music as the other, what to teach becomes more obvious.

	Melody	Duration	Form	Tempo	Timbre	Dynamics	Simultaneous Sounds
Sing							
Play							
Move							
Read							
Write							
Listen							
Create							

The questions then become

> How can I teach about melody (form, dynamics)
> through singing?
> through moving?
> through listening?

One aspect of melody may be approached in many different ways, through the seven basic activities. The children may sing the song, showing with hand levels where the sounds go higher and where lower and where they repeat; they may move around the room in a way that illustrates melodic contour; they may carry the melody to the xylophone and play it in higher and lower places; they may listen to a recording of it and discuss the ways in which it is the same as or different from their own rendition; they may diagram the melodic contour; they may follow its notation in music books; they may create a melodic ostinato to accompany it.

Each musical element may be thought of in the same way in terms of the seven basic musical activities. The teaching possibilities become almost limitless when looked at in this way. To make them more manageable, we need instructional objectives for each grade.

Instructional Objectives

Instructional objectives are a bit like goals. They indicate where we want to go. However, they are shorter term and more specific. All our instructional objectives should be related to one or another of our overall goals as well as to the age and experience of the children. A specific instructional objective may be written for one lesson:

> "The children will diagram the form of 'Hot Cross Buns' using felt shapes, squares, and circles and will use the words *same* and *different* to describe the phrases."

It may be written more broadly to involve several lessons:

> "The children will diagram the form of six of their simple songs using felt shapes and letter designations. They will aurally identify which phrases are the same, which are different, and which are similar in these songs."

Instructional objectives usually are directly related to one musical element but may involve several musical activities. In the preceding objective, the element to be studied was form, but the activities obviously implied were singing, listening, and writing (or constructing). They could easily have been increased to include moving ("change direction on the *b* phrase"), playing instruments ("play only the *a* phrases"), and creating ("make up two four-beat rhythm patterns; arrange them in *aaba* form").

Before writing instructional objectives, it is helpful to list the following:

1. What element am I working on?
2. What new concept (understanding) do I want the children to infer about this element?
3. What skill(s) are to be developed as we learn about this?
4. What concepts (understandings) must the children already have when we begin? What skills?

In writing the instructional objective, consider these things:

1. Who will do the action: the children
2. What the action will be:

>   Will sing the song
>
>   Will step the beat
>
>   Will show the melodic contour
>
>   Will play the tune on their recorders
>
>   Will read the new song
>
>   Will notate the phrase
>
>   Will create an ostinato
>
>   Will identify the form, etc.

3. What the musical material(s) will be:

>   Six folksongs (list the specific ones)
>
>   Examples from their recorder books (specific examples)
>
>   Romanze from *Eine kleine Nachtmusik*

4. How the teacher (or children) will decide whether the task has been successfully accomplished (what constitutes an acceptable performance): if it has been done

>   Accurately
>
>   In tune
>
>   At the pitch given by the teacher
>
>   On the first try
>
>   Given two chances

Using instructional objectives as the basis for planning has the advantage that assessment is built in. They are stated in clear behavioral terms that leave no doubt as to what outcome is expected.

If one writes instructional objectives broadly enough to encompass a number of lessons, then there should be more than one such objective per lesson. In one half-hour music class, the children might be working on as many as four objectives, and certainly over a period of a month, objectives in each element should be included in lesson plans.

ACTIVITIES

1. Write one instructional objective for each element of music. Be sure that the objectives you write are congruent with the goals you wrote.

2. Take one of the foregoing objectives and describe how it could be implemented with each of the seven basic musical activities.

LESSON PLANNING

Although it is important to know what one wishes to see as a final outcome of music education (philosophy and goals) and where one hopes to be by January (instructional objectives), the burning question for most beginning teachers is "What shall I teach next Tuesday?" For this, a simple lesson-plan form is recommended. The top should show the grade level, the date, and the instructional objectives being worked on. The body includes the musical materials to be used within the lesson, in teaching order, with accompanying activities. The bottom is a checklist so that certain kinds of experiences are not neglected.

A form such as this can be prepared for several weeks or for half a year ahead, with only the center portion left free to fill in weekly. It has the advantage that one's objectives are always in front of one, while the actual means to achieve those objectives can be chosen with children's needs in mind from week to week.

LESSON PLAN FORM

Grade   Date

Instructional Objectives
    Melody
    Duration
    Form
    Tempo
    Timbre
    Dynamics
    Simultaneous Sounds

LESSON #
Song or Musical Material   Activities
    1.
    2.
    3.
    4.
    5.

Check activities used

    Singing   Writing or constructing
    Playing instruments   Listening
    Moving   Creating
    Reading

Not every activity will be included every week. Not every instructional objective for a six-week period will be touched on in every lesson. However, over a period of a semester, most will have been covered, and over a period of years, far more will be taught and learned than is likely without such planning.

ACTIVITIES

Fill out lesson planning charts for one lesson in grade one and for one lesson in grade four. Tell what background your imaginary children bring to these lessons (entry-level musical concepts and skills).

PLANNING FOR PROGRAMS

Twice a year, usually in December and May, the mind of even the most unmusical of administrators suddenly awakens to the existence (or lack) of music in his or her school. It is time for "*the* program." Few principals are unaware of the public relations value of music, even if they are unsure of its educational value.

If there is no professional music teacher in the building, any teacher who can play a little piano or who has been overheard singing with children is fair game.

"Miss Jones, would you please get together a little program for the parent-teachers meeting in three weeks? I thought you could put together a little chorus. They could meet before school or on your lunch hour." If that request seems laughable, it is, nevertheless, not uncommon.

If you are responsible for the music in a school, or even if you are not responsible but have taken a music course or two and do not see anyone else taking the responsibility for getting children ready to perform in programs, take the responsibility yourself! You will probably end up with it, anyway.

By assuming the responsibility for programs in advance, you have an enormous advantage—you can work on them in a civilized manner all year instead of working on them frantically for three weeks. Perhaps, with a well-laid plan and a frontal attack on the principal's office, you may even get a scheduled time weekly for choir rehearsals that does not necessitate getting up at dawn or missing meals.

If rehearsal time is approached as teaching time, it is much easier to justify making it a part of the school day. The idea that performance is the principal goal of music education and that it doesn't really matter how that performance is achieved is becoming increasingly passé. Neither knowledgeable administrators nor parents will be satisfied today with the band or choir that can perform three tunes but knows nothing about music.

Today, music educators realize that the ability and knowledge acquired in preparation for a performance may far outlast the memory of the performance itself. A choir or an instrumental ensemble should be learning music through the rehearsal process, not just learning pieces. The *process* of rehearsal is more important than the product. Performance should carry with it musical understanding.

Choosing the Choir

It is best if you do not choose a choir at the elementary level. Choosing automatically implies that some children are not chosen. A ten-year-old who doesn't "make" choir may carry scars forever from the experience. Whole-class, whole-grade, or double-grade choirs are a reasonable alternative. Everybody in both classes of grade five could become the choir for the Winter Program, while all classes of grade six could sing in the Spring Program. If the school is small, the choir could be everyone in grades four, five, and six. This arrangement has the additional advantage that material for programs could be worked on both in music periods and at rehearsal times.

If, as sometimes happens, school policy demands a smaller, cross-grade choir, there should be a sign-up sheet with children taken on a first-come basis. That way, the choir is made up of those children who really want to be in it. A "waiting list" can be made of the children who sign up below the agreed-upon number.

Getting into choir should be easy. Staying in choir should be difficult. There should be stringent rules for the running of rehearsals—procedures for entering and leaving the rehearsal room in an orderly fashion, for picking up music, for taking attendance, for dealing with tardy choir members. Anyone who misses two choir rehearsals for a reason other than illness should have to give up his or her place to the next person on the waiting list. The children should know the rules, and the rules should be applied impartially. It is not as easy to teach a 60- or 100-voice choir as it is to teach a class of 25 students. It is important to establish standards for behavior in choir at the first rehearsal.

Of course, it is possible to work with a smaller group, but the larger number will make part singing easier and more secure. In addition, in an unselected choir there are likely to be children with pitch problems. A greater mass of voices both helps these children and tends to somewhat disguise imperfections. One wonderful side effect of allowing such children into the choir is that often, by performance time, they can sing in tune. Whether it is the extra emphasis on singing or the motivation of approaching performance that causes this, it happens too regularly to be an accident.

Rehearsals should be planned as thoroughly as lessons. Which pieces will you practice? How much time will you devote to each? On what aspect of each piece will you be focusing?

The pieces on which you intend to work should be listed in rehearsal order on the chalkboard so that choir members can have their music ready at the beginning of the rehearsal. Warm-up exercises, scales sung on open vowels, are a good way to begin a rehearsal.

Choosing Music

Music for the choir may be chosen from a variety of sources and should range from easy to challenging, with more pieces at the easy to middle level than at the difficult level. Working very intensively on one piece may be interesting and rewarding; having to work intensively on five pieces is generally frustrating to both children and teacher.

Ten to twelve pieces of music are usually enough for a children's school concert. One of these might be a difficult two- or three-part octavo composition or arrangement. Three or four could be canons or rounds. Three others could involve simple descants, and the remaining numbers could be unison with and without accompaniment. Opportunities should be found for several children to sing small solo parts, a phrase or a verse of a song.[6]

At least some music should be unaccompanied, and even pieces that call for instrumental accompaniment should be taught initially without, to ensure better intonation.

Parents tend to be an uncritical audience. Nevertheless, for the sake of children performing, the teacher should aim for the most polished performance possible. Children know when they have performed well and when they have not. A simple piece sung with musicality and understanding will contribute far more to children's aesthetic development than showier numbers sung less well. The choir experience should exist for the education of the children, not for the amusement of the audience.[7]

SO YOU STILL WANT TO TEACH MUSIC

Teaching elementary school music is one of the most frustrating, exhausting jobs in the entire field of education. There is rarely enough time allowed in the schedule; many schools do not even have graded music textbooks; fewer still have such other supplies as might be needed—octavo music for choir, a good sound system, a properly equipped music room, classroom instruments, a decent piano.

Luckily, aside from the first of these—time—none of the rest is really necessary to a good music program. All that is necessary is a musical teacher and some children. Because if teaching music is one of the most frustrating jobs in the school, it is also one of the most satisfying. The expressions on children's faces as they sing a loved song, as they move through the steps of a favorite folk dance, as they listen to a known recording—these are the rewards for teaching music. Music has the capacity to touch the human spirit in a way no other subject does.